The Asperger Social Guide

How to relate with confidence
to anyone in any social situation
as an adult with Asperger's syndrome

Genevieve Edmonds and Dean Worton

P·C·P
Paul Chapman
Publishing

A Lucky Duck Book

Paul Chapman Publishing
A SAGE Publications Company
1 Oliver's Yard
55 City Road
London EC1Y 1SP

SAGE Publications Inc.
2455 Teller Road
Thousand Oaks, California 91320

SAGE Publications India Pvt Ltd
B-42, Panchsheel Enclave
Post Box 4109
New Delhi 110 017

www.luckyduck.co.uk

Commissioning Editor: Barbara Maines
Editorial Team: Wendy Ogden, Sarah Lynch, Mel Maines
Designer: Jess Wright
Photographs: Andrew Bailey

A catalogue record for this book is available from the British Library

Library of Congress Control Number 2006901496

ISBN 13 978-1-4129-2023-0   ISBN 13 978-1-4129-2024-7 (pbk)
ISBN 10 1-4129-2023-X   ISBN 10 1-4129-2024-8 (pbk)

Printed on paper from sustainable resources
Printed in Great Britain by The Cromwell Press Ltd, Trowbridge, Wiltshire

About the authors

Genevieve Edmonds is a 25 year old with 'residual' Asperger's syndrome, which she views as a significant gift. She works as an associate of the Missing Link Support Service Ltd. in Lancashire supporting those 'disabled by society' including individuals with ASD. She speaks and writes frequently in the field of Autism, along with giving training, workshops and soon counselling. She aims to empower those with ASD, carers and professionals in the understanding of Asperger's syndrome as a difference rather than an impairment. She lives and works in a solution-focused way and is based in north-west England.

Dean Worton is a 33 year old high functioning individual with a very positive expression of Asperger syndrome. He runs a very successful UK-based website for adults with Asperger's syndrome and hosts real life meet-ups around the UK for its members. His key interest is in encouraging adults to live positively and successfully with the gifts that Asperger's syndrome provides. He also works in administration and resides in north-west England.

Dedications

Genevieve: To my sister, Fiona, for your individuality and eccentricity. Also for being a great supporter.

Dean: To members of Aspie Village for your loyalty.

Acknowledgements

Luke Beardon, again, for your pertinent foreword and just for being you.

Andrew, for being so patient and surviving taking our photos for us – much appreciation.

Contents

Foreword

The second in a series of three, *The Asperger's Social Guide* follows on from *The Asperger's Love Guide* and precedes *The Asperger's Personal Guide*. While I have yet to read the third guide I can confidently recommend *The Asperger's Social Guide* to all people with autism/Asperger's syndrome as an insightful and potentially hugely beneficial text to support everyday life.

It constantly amazes me just how much the NT person takes for granted: the innate ability to social chit-chat; the ease with which we communicate with one another; the way in which we can enter a social situation and within seconds have a good understanding of how we should behave. However, any people with Asperger's syndrome find the social world a chaotic maze without a handy map supplied to help guide their way. Far too often people with AS are left without even a rudimentary set of directions, let alone a detailed map. What Gen and Dean have supplied goes some way towards rectifying that situation, and it is with great pleasure and a sense of privilege that I am introducing The Asperger's Social Guide.

There are abundant texts on autism and AS written by individuals, parents, and 'professionals'. The insight that both Gen and Dean have into their own autism, combined with their genuine personalities and willingness and abilities to support other people with AS, means that The Asperger's Social Guide is not only useful for people with autism, but for everyone who is involved in the field. It provides hugely supportive suggestions for how people with AS can develop their skills, as well as a superb insight into the lives of people with autism. It is for these reasons that I would recommend it not only for people with autism/AS, but to anyone who wants to gain a deeper understanding of the needs of people on the autistic spectrum.

I was chatting to a young woman the other day who was very bright and articulate, and she had a fantastic way of expressing herself. She told me that socially it feels as though she is dragging around a ball and chain – but it is invisible so no one else knows it's there. It seems to me a wonderful way of explaining how problematic life can be for someone with AS, and yet the problems are often so invisible that support is not readily available, and is often lacking altogether. At present support mechanisms around social support are generally woeful, to the detriment of people with AS. Such lack of support should never be taken lightly – it can easily lead to major problems for the individual. With The Asperger's Social Guide, the authors have provided a detailed social map, while acknowledging that all social situations are potentially problematic and the world is not an ideal place. It is a considerable accomplishment that they have tackled such a complex issue, and produced such a readable, insightful and beneficial guide.

I have huge admiration for Gen and Dean as individuals, and great envy at their ability to present such an excellent publication. I would like to thank them for allowing me the opportunity to write this foreword, and to allow me to be a part of their lives.

Luke Beardon
Senior Lecturer in Autism, Sheffield Hallam university

Introduction

'I have a degree from the university of Life.' This is a phrase which is often said jokingly, however for many people with AS it might be less of a joke. A degree from the university of Life might be well received by many people with AS! Often for individuals with AS the academic side of life is relatively straightforward – it is the everyday social world that is the great struggle. Wouldn't it be nice if there were a degree available in 'the everyday social world'? Sadly it would be virtually impossible to put together such a course.

More is now known about how Asperger's syndrome affects individuals than ever before. However, how does this knowledge translate into supporting the everyday social lives of the adult individuals with Asperger's syndrome? Individuals with Asperger's syndrome often struggle to make sense of, and relate to, the everyday world we all have to live in. Knowing how to relate in everyday life to the never-ending amount of social situations and many different people an individual comes across can be a minefield of utter confusion. However, getting by socially is the key to most things in life, and to survival. Even the most basic everyday situation is often complicated by social issues.

This guide aims to help with that. Written from the perspective of two high functioning Asperger's adults the guide covers many social situations in which those without autism take for granted in knowing what to do and how to behave. It is a practical pick-up-and-use guide for individuals with Asperger's syndrome (and other ASDs) to use in their daily lives to make their way in a very confusing social world (which they cannot easily opt out of) and to have a decent quality of life.

We have tried to put together tips and strategies for coping every day in the social world. In writing the guide it further emphasised for us just how hard it is to quantify and write down social rules. There are so many factors affecting these rules, such as context, time, culture, situation, mood, physical state, gender, race and so on. There are simply no 100% correct social rules. It would be impossible to ever make them as the social world is simply not logical or factual. In some ways, for an Aspie, this could be seen as a positive thing, in that since there is no one correct way to behave it is easier to be 'oneself'. However, sadly society expects certain conduct that is unwritten, yet this is changeable and not always definable. How unfair!

Despite this we still felt that writing the guide was a worthwhile exercise. It is a good starting point from which to think about social rules, their importance and how to meaningfully employ them to get by in everyday life. For some people with AS, some of the guide may appear very patronising or 'stating the obvious', yet for others it may be very welcome. Some of it may appear very simplistic, some of it more complicated. Of course, all Aspies are highly individual, so we tried to be as broad and basic as possible to cater for all levels and abilities. Our aim with the guide is to provide some basic pointers which in our experience have worked. This is a guide that can be picked up at times of high anxiety, or at times of over-analytical and over-complicating thought, when philosophising takes over, and basic rules that you knew all along are forgotten, or mistrusted! Naturally, a personal interpretation of the social world takes into account personal values. Therefore, it is open to interpretation and not to be taken as 'gospel'! We hope that individuals with AS or others ASDs will use it as a starting point from which they can make their own interpretation of the social world, to take as little or as much from the book as they find helpful. Although the title of this book states 'Asperger' individuals we feel it can be used by all individuals on the autistic spectrum with or without support.

Naturally we couldn't possibly have been able to cover every social situation or we would never have finished writing the guide! We have covered situations which we felt were very general. However, caution needs to be taken due to the fact that no one social situation is ever the same each time around! Context is always going to be very relevant, so always take this into account. The best way to learn socially is by experience. Everybody, not just people on the autistic spectrum, experiences social confusion and uncertainty over what society expects of them, so take heart! The difference with autistic people is that they may learn in a more concrete, direct and scientific way. This is OK too, but perhaps requires more effort in a social world, which isn't designed for autistic people.

In writing the guide we both learnt new social relating concepts from the other, refreshed our current knowledge, and complicated our previous social knowledge, so it has been a learning curve for both of us!

A note on terminology used in this guide

Aspie – This refers to an able high-functioning individual with Asperger's syndrome. However, the book can be used by lower functioning individuals on the autistic spectrum with support from a support worker, carer, parent or trusted friend.

NTs – a term used for the purposes of writing referring to mainstream neurologically 'normal' (neurotypical) individuals.

AS – short for Asperger's syndrome.

ASD – short for Autistic Spectrum Disorder.

Autistic – covering people on the whole autistic spectrum including people with Asperger's syndrome, High Functioning Autism and Classic Autism.

Stims – Self-stimulatory behaviour: repetitive motor or vocal mannerism engaged in by people with ASDs. They are usually used to either calm or excite the nervous system and often as a response to strong emotion.

Chapter 1

Asperger's Syndrome and Relating to People

Playing the social game

'Game playing' is something that Aspies are not supposed to be natural at. Yet a lot of what makes the social world go round is this concept of 'playing the game', that is, doing what it takes to get by socially. One of the great things about Aspies is their strong sense of social justice, equality and fairness. However, the social world does not appear to revolve around these beliefs. It seems that in order to have success in the social world you have to be willing to be a 'player', which often compromises equality and fairness.

One way to get around this as an Aspie is to try and meet the social world 'halfway'; i.e. retain your basic self-beliefs, but play along a bit with the majority to get by. In fact, play them at their own game! This could be translated practically into following the unwritten social rules that are essential to ensure your own safety, the safety of others, having pleasant and polite social relations and integrating into society in some form which makes you reasonable happy and satisfied in life. What needs to happen is that society is shown that you respect the 'majority' ways of being; but that society equally accepts Aspie ways of being.

Getting along with yourself

Too many Aspies make the mistake of thinking that they are inferior or worthless just because that is the way other ignorant people usually seem to view them. The thing to remember is that everyone is different and you are allowed to be the person that you are. If you're not hurting others or yourself, no one has the right to criticise your character. People who don't give you a chance in life are simply not worth it. Everyone has strengths and qualities. Some people with Asperger's syndrome will say that that isn't true of them, but in actual fact anyone who says that of themselves is nearly always being too hard on themselves.

Some Aspies are perfectionists. No wonder this causes depression because, as the saying goes, nobody is perfect. It doesn't matter that you are different from the majority of people. This is only a problem because the way the majority live life is thought by that majority to be the only way to be, but the reality is that this is only because they don't understand different ways of 'being'. This is only because they are not used to people acting unlike the majority of people. However, this does not make the behaviour of people with Asperger's syndrome wrong and in many cases people with Asperger's syndrome have a sensible approach to life, such as following rules and doing things correctly. Slip-ups may be caused by less sensible people taking advantage of the better nature of people with Asperger's syndrome.

It could well be that even though you don't know it yet that you're a much better person than you think you are and don't be fooled if you've had lots of ill treatment from people. If you approach people in a pleasant way, then you already have something to be proud of and should like yourself. In fact, sometimes getting along with yourself will help other people to get on with you better too.

Having a positive outlook

Although this may be difficult if bad experiences keep occurring, for Aspies, life is a steep learning curve and gradually bad experiences can be reduced. Don't expect to stop having bad experiences altogether. The important thing is that in time your bad experiences will be outweighed by your good experiences and you'll be much happier, which will give you confidence and you can then start to get on with yourself. This is all about avoiding 'all or nothing' thinking. Just because a person might not have all the things right in their life at one time, it doesn't mean that this is the only way it will ever be – the grey areas in between are just as acceptable. Having a well-balanced outlook means that social relating can become easier since having an extreme attitude in any sense makes it very hard for others to relate in a reasonable way to such a person.

It is unhealthy for anyone to live their life by comparison with other people. You could be thinking about what is good about you and what you can do to make a difference in the world and make someone happy. Life is not just about being born, working, having relationships, starting a family and dying. Although most people do wish to do all of these things, it is not good to allow your whole mind to be dictated by this. You could concentrate on living your own life and not a life that is better or comparable with someone else.

Many people would like a life partner and children one day and people with Asperger's syndrome are often depressed because these things take so much longer before they happen to them. However, there are no deadlines on how soon you should have a partner, be married, start a family and so on. Life is not a race. If you are in your twenties and have never had a relationship or only been in relationships briefly there is nothing abnormal about this, and people who make you feel that there is do not have the right to speak to you in such a way. It is extremely disrespectful and narrow-minded of them. There is plenty of time for relationships when you are in your thirties. We are not suggesting that you should not have relationships before then. We are merely suggesting that if you are in your twenties and have not yet been in a serious relationship then don't obsess greatly over it. It is much better to think about relationships as little as possible and if a relationship does comes along that is wonderful, but in the meantime try to concentrate on simply doing something positive with your life.

This could be related to your job. If you haven't yet achieved the job role or career you hoped for, you obsess over this to the detriment of everything else and so relating socially becomes difficult. If you are not employed, a good idea is to take up voluntary work. This does not just include all the traditional types that would spring to mind such as caring for people. There is a whole host of voluntary positions, for example, practical work or administration. Your local Job Centre should be able to put you in touch with an organisation which matches people up with volunteering opportunities. Volunteering is very rewarding. It is putting something back into the community and gives you something to be proud of yourself for.

Keeping your outlook as positive as possible is a basis upon which to relate well with others as negativity often makes relations strained and difficult. It doesn't mean that you would need to go around with an unrealistic outlook as nobody can be positive all the time, but trying to be constructively positive makes relations easier for everyone.

Look after yourself

It is also a good idea to look after yourself. Naturally, the better you feel, the better you will be able to put energy and effort into relating well with others. For example, it is a good idea to eat all the 'right' foods. Many with Asperger's syndrome have a different metabolism and perhaps cannot afford to be as carefree in their diet as NTs. You could consult publications for more information about Asperger's diets. A good place to start is the Internet, just type 'Asperger's and diet' into any good search engine. Also, take a lot of exercise and maintain the routine. Anxiety seems to occur a lot with AS, and exercise is a great way of keeping excess anxiety away. Exercising is a great way to keep both body and mind in balance and isn't just about looking good!

If there is anything to do with your health and fitness that you are concerned about, try to consult your GP about it or have a general check-up. Mentioning AS to your GP, even if they may not have the best knowledge of it, is still worthwhile. A good choice of supplement for people with Asperger's syndrome is Omega 3 Fish Oils, which should be available from all health food shops. Other good supplements are flax-seed oil, evening primrose oil, folic acid and a good multivitamin and mineral supplement. Check with a pharmacist which supplements are right for you.

Positive coping strategies

You might be wondering how this is relevant to relating to people. Well, in order to relate well to people it is helpful to be sound of mind and therefore sound of body. Therefore, it is crucial to take care of yourself. Do what works!

For example, people with Asperger's syndrome can be absent-minded, and they need to get into the habit of writing out reminders. Some Aspies have even gone as far as leaving notes all over their house. You may think that this sounds crazy, but the reality is that nothing is crazy if it improves your standard of life in any way. Something as small as that can make a huge impact on your lifestyle. Of course, you may not be welcome to post notes all around the house, but you can at least put reminders in your bedroom. You can buy Post-it notes (usually they are yellow, but other colours are now available) and use those. It would be useful to have Post-it notes of as many different colours as possible as that way, different colours can relate to different themes. It would be a good idea to write on the notes in felt-tip colour pens to make them stand out more. You could also purchase a cork notice board that you can put little pieces of paper onto with drawing pins. Of course, these won't necessarily help when you are out and about somewhere and you may need to remember things for when you get home.

A good strategy might be to always carry a book with you to write things down in. Also, having a diary is a great help. All of these things may sound obvious but many Aspies cope well with visual supports and the examples we have outlined relate to this. Finding individual coping strategies is best.

It may all sound like a chore, but once coping strategies are put into place, they become easy to maintain because eventually you will use the system automatically without thinking.

If you are wondering again how all of the above is relevant to relating to people, it all helps because having problems with remembering to do things can be a source of great stress and anxiety and this can make it far more difficult for people to relate to you. This is one example of how coping strategies for specific issues, such an as memory problems, can make a big impact on getting by in everyday life.

If you can manage to get problem areas under control using coping strategies such as those suggested above, stress and anxiety will become gradually reduced. In turn this will improve your mental health and wellbeing and because you will be happier, you will be a better person to be around because if you like yourself then other people will too.

Confidence

Mental wellbeing also involves feeling confident in yourself. The more comfortable and self-assured you feel, the more able you will feel to tackle life's social expectations. The key is to get the right balance of confidence. There is a big difference between being aggressive and being assertive. When you are aggressive, it makes you come across in an unpleasant and often intimidating way, which is of course totally unnecessary. Another way of describing how a person can be assertive is to say he stands up for himself. Standing up for yourself does not mean being violent or aggressive. There is no need to shout at people in order to stand up for yourself. It is better not to shout at people unless it cannot be avoided, nor do you need to be defensive. All you need to do is state your case clearly and if someone is insulting to you, instead of reacting in an emotional way such as being angry or upset with them, you would be better to react in an unconcerned way. You could do this either by ignoring them, shrugging, laughing it off or just calmly agreeing with them. For example, if they say, 'You are a complete idiot,' you could reply with, 'Really? I didn't know that,' 'Thanks for sharing that with me,' or 'Yeah, I know,' with a smile, although not in a meek way, just be nonchalant with them. This will most likely ruin the person's fun or malicious intent and you can stay in control and keep your confidence.

If you are intelligent, caring and kind to people, which people who insult you clearly are not, then you keep telling yourself this. This is likely to make you feel a lot better about yourself and it will become easier to be more relaxed in the company of others. If you are in a group of people that includes a difficult person, try just to let it wash over you. Who knows, you might even start to relate well to that person. People have been known to become best friends with their tormenters, although we are not suggesting that this is always appropriate in every case.

Be your own best friend

Perhaps a further aid to getting on with yourself is to treat yourself as you would a good friend. Giving yourself a break from constant self-criticism and perfectionist thought is essential for wellbeing. Treat yourself well. Being good to yourself as opposed to being hard on yourself will give you more confidence about getting on with others.

As a person with Asperger's syndrome you may well have been bullied a lot in life, not necessarily just in your schooldays but also in your adult life. Adults tend not to use physical bullying as much as children do, so the type of bullying you may suffer at present is probably verbal, which is just as humiliating and damaging. Be aware that the people doing this have their own problems, which they are attempting to disguise by singling you out. In fact, they probably have low self-esteem themselves. Certainly it is best not to concern yourself too much with such people. Why should anyone who treats others like that receive respect? Try not to 'feed' these people with reasons to treat you this way. You need to make it boring for them by not allowing them to get to you, as difficult as this may seem. A useful method to not let it get to you when they make verbal remarks is to form a ridiculous picture in your head, such as one of them wearing silly clothes and looking humiliated. If you imagine them looking like a clown, that is quite appropriate for their personality. Chances are you are much better than these people and do not let anyone tell you any differently! Everyone has strengths and weaknesses, so you should concentrate on your strengths. Other people may think they are better because they have more strengths in social situations and many people in high-up positions are there because they are good at dealing with people. There is a saying 'There are those who can talk a good job, and those who can do a good job'. Sometimes people with Asperger's syndrome would be able to do many aspects of such a job better than the appointed person, but people are often recruited not only for their knowledge but for their social skills.

Empathy

Be aware of empathy. This is not the Aspie strong point, but no matter what social situation you are in, or how you are interacting, empathy forms a baseline for successful relating. When someone does not have empathy this indicates that they assume that everyone else knows what they know, or that others cannot have another point of view than their own.

For example, a man from Scotland with Asperger's syndrome called John is visiting London and starts talking to a man in a pub he's never met before. The man asks John where he works. He states, 'I work at Patel's Newsagents on Fisher Street near Junction 12 of the M8.' If John had thought it through, he would probably have thought on about the fact that a random person in London is unlikely to have ever heard of that newsagents or street. Even if the man is good on Scottish geography, which he probably is not, he is very unlikely to be able to differentiate between all the motorway junctions in Scotland! Perhaps all he wanted to know, for the purpose of 'small talk', was a basic answer such as, 'I work at a newsagents up in Scotland.' Though at the same time, you should try not to state the obvious to people too much.

Trying to consider everything from another person's point of view when interacting with them is a great rule of thumb. Naturally you cannot be psychic, and dwelling too much on trying to guess their point of view is mind-boggling! Lacking in empathy too, can in some cases wreck successful social relating. If your AS affects you in such a way that you are able to learn to look at yourself and accept that you need more support to empathise, this is the first and most important step to coping with the way you are. It doesn't appear that a person with AS can 'learn' empathy, but it does appear that having support in learning the best way you can to empathise is possible.

AS and self-awareness

Some Aspies have an excellent understanding of how AS affects them. This may be because it happens to be one of their interests, or have decided it would be a worthwhile task in order to understand themselves better. However, most people on the autistic spectrum seem to find introspection (self-analysis) very difficult. This may be due to many Aspies excelling in concrete, logical thought rather than abstract thinking involving emotions and less rational concepts. However, having an awareness of how AS affects you individually is very important. This is for a variety of reasons but in this context the benefits translate directly into relating successfully to others.

Comparing yourself with NTs and how they relate is not always a helpful exercise, since being an Aspie is often described as 'coming from another planet'. Therefore, it would be as silly as an NT trying to work themselves out based on an autistic framework. This is not to suggest that Asperger's syndrome becomes the reason behind everything, or everything you do, say or think is down to you being an Aspie. It is about gleaning as much input as you can about AS, and trying to work out how AS might affect you in a certain situation. It is not going to be possible to attribute with any certainty how much AS affects you in various circumstances. Certainty is not the goal here, but having a well-rounded self-awareness.

Therefore, try to glean as much information as you can about AS: read the literature, talk to others with AS, online or in real life, have sessions with an AS knowledgeable counsellor… do what works to gain a picture of how AS might affect you.

Explaining your AS to others

We will cover this briefly in relation to specific social situations later in this book. The ability to explain how your AS affects you to others is a very useful skill to have. However, don't make the mistake of lecturing anyone and everyone you meet about Asperger's syndrome and how it affects you. It is a very individual choice whether you disclose your AS, how much of the details and to whom. However, there may be times when you are required to explain how AS affects you and certainly giving an individual picture of how AS affects you can be essential where even professionals often cling tightly to very stereotypical views of AS which are not relevant to such individual people. Beware of how you phrase things when you do explain AS. In a society where any 'mental' differences are often given blanket connotations which include fear, danger and crime, choosing more neutral and positive words will certainly help if explaining AS either to someone who knows nothing and someone who thinks they know it all about autism. Always assert yourself, and never, ever give in to people talking about AS and autism in ways you are not happy with.

Over-analysis and social obsessing

Having to pick your way through the social world through intellect, having to analyse social exchanges, having to weigh up what to do and what to say all the time is exhausting. Not only is it exhausting, but it can also, at times, draw an autistic person further away from reality. By this we mean it is easy to mistrust everything people do and say or how you could lose your basic sense of self, emotions and individuality when striving to 'go with the flow'. It is easy to become fragmented in your behaviour, obsessing all the time over socially acceptable behaviour. Becoming fragmented means that even the simplest interaction can become over-analysed to the point that high anxiety levels can occur. Try to keep this in check, and remember that you still need to have trust in your basic emotional instincts in social interactions.

Dealing with anger and emotional difficulties

We will cover this topic in much more depth in The Asperger's Personal Guide. However, it is relevant to mention it in terms of relating well socially. It is quite possible that as an adult with Asperger's syndrome you will have had your fair share of emotional problems to deal with in life, and as a result you may have suffered depression, anxiety and anger. There is a temptation when relating to others with and without AS to somehow, often subconsciously, to make them a scapegoat (target) for how unfairly you may have been treated in the past. This is perfectly understandable, since people with AS tend to know more about this then the average NT.

Hard as it may be, no matter how frustrated you feel with others, in order to relate well with them, you need to be able to keep your emotions balanced. The right places to vent emotions are with a counsellor or supporter who is OK with this. If you are going through a phase where you are feeling particularly stressed, unhappy or angry it may be better to limit times when you have to relate to others socially. It is about getting the right balance of offloading your emotions in the right environment and trying to keep them under control at other times. Society expects that in most situations you will keep your emotions as neutral as possible, except in very specific situations, such as funerals.

No matter how bad you feel, society does not take kindly to people who show their feelings publicly. This is deemed inappropriate. This is a tough lesson to learn, and all the more soul-destroying when you feel stressed a lot of the time. The best way to influence others is by being constructive and non-emotional. If you feel that you cannot control your anger or emotions, it may be that there is an underlying cause that may be helped by appropriate medication or therapeutic intervention. This is something which you should discuss with an appropriate medical professional.

It seems that half of the battle is that the basic social needs that humans have are never going to be easily met with a 'difference', and the fight is dealing with the frustration and sadness that not having these met can bring, rather than the AS itself.

Chapter 2

Communication and Ways of Relating

Ways of relating

What is 'relating' anyway? Words that come to mind are 'connect', or 'link'. For the context of this book we are referring to the ability to connect socially to both people and situations. In order to relate socially, it is necessary to 'communicate' the information needed and then exchange it appropriately with the person or within the social situation. Sounds complicated? If you are on the autistic spectrum it is complicated further. However, that does not mean that relating well is not an option if you are on the autistic spectrum. It just means that more thought and direct learning might have to be put into relating. That is not to say that all NTs find it easy either.

We know that Aspies do not always communicate brilliantly in verbal or non-verbal interaction. Some Aspies learn and improve their verbal and non-verbal communication skills and can become quite adept at it. Others still struggle. Thankfully there is more than one way to relate. The key is to find a way that works best for you and to capitalise on this. In this chapter we cover a number of ways to relate socially.

The telephone

Using the telephone can be a bit traumatic for some Aspies. It is best to think what you want to get across and/or what you want to find out. You could always write keyword notes before you make the call. For some people, writing out a script of what you're going to say could help, although you should only rely on this if all else fails.

If you're phoning a company then perhaps have written down in front of you any names, reference codes etc. that you may be asked for. This will prevent the anxiety of being asked for a piece of information that you may have to go to a different part of the house to look for, and so you can be a bit more relaxed.

There is no need to panic when you start to explain the purpose of your call. If the person on the other end is impatient with you, then they are probably like that all the time anyway, so it is unlikely to be your fault. However, many people are pleasant and are only willing to help.

When you make a call you should ask for the person you wish to speak to or to speak to someone that deals with whatever it is you're ringing about. Always be polite and don't start and end without saying, 'Hello', 'Goodbye' and 'Thank you'.

If you are answering the call, you should pick up the phone and say, 'Hello.' Again, you should remain polite and if the call is for someone else say, 'Hold on, I'll just get him/her.' If that person is unavailable or not in say, 'I'll let him/her know you've called, could I take a message?' Make sure that you write the message clearly and that you pass it on to the person it is for as soon as you see them or call them to let them know if it is an urgent message. In all phone calls speak as slowly and clearly as possible, otherwise it could cause problems and therefore anxiety.

If it becomes apparent that the person on the other end has the wrong number, do not be impolite to them. Although you may feel annoyed because someone wasted your time with a call that was not intended for your phone, do not forget that we have all dialled the wrong number before and the person will be surprised that they happened to ring the wrong number. Simply say, 'Sorry, I think you must have the wrong number,' and if they apologise say, 'That's OK, bye.'

Whether you are making or receiving the call, also pay attention to the length of the call. The telephone is not the best medium by which to relate a long story as it is expensive and someone else may be trying to get through. In a telephone conversation try to simply make a summary of the key points. If you are asked a question which it is impossible to give a quick answer to it is better to say, 'It's a long story, I'll tell you when we meet up.' That is unless of course you would prefer to relate it over the phone, in which case be mindful of your own or the other person's phone bill!

Writing to people

This varies greatly according to whom you are writing. If you are writing to a friend or relative, as a minimum you should put your address and the date at the top of the letter so that they can reply. Even if they are likely to know your address, still include it as they may well forget it one day and if they rely on an address book, they might lose it and therefore your address.

Formal letters

If you are writing to someone other than a friend, there is a letter writing etiquette. Usually you would address them by their title, i.e. Dear Mr Smith, Dear Dr Smith, etc. If they are female and you don't know their title, use Ms, i.e. Dear Ms Smith. You would always do this for most formal letters, such as job applications. This applies even if you are related to the person to whom you're writing. In some business letters, it is fine to use the person's first name if you have established first name terms with them, though the company you work for may insist on you always using the person's title in correspondence. If in doubt, always use the person's title. You then end the letter with 'Yours sincerely' followed by your name. If you don't know the persons name always start with Dear Sir/Madam and end with 'Yours faithfully'.

A model formal letter

David Jones

1 High Street

London

W1 1AA

1 January 2006

Mr A Smith

Personnel Manager

ABC Products Ltd

1 Oxford Street

London

W1 2AA

Dear Mr Smith

Would it be possible for you to send me an application form for the position of Administrative Assistant, which was advertised in today's Daily Herald? I look forward to your reply.

Yours sincerely

(Your signature goes here)

Dean Worton

NB If you don't know the person's name, change Mr Smith to Sir/Madam and Yours sincerely to Yours faithfully.

Informal letters

If you are sending someone a postcard, it will usually be someone that you are on informal terms with. If you are sending it to the place where you work, then ensure that it's polite and avoid providing too many personal details so that you do not face disciplinary action when you get back or worse still leave yourself with no job to go back to! Avoid the temptation to write too much on a postcard, as otherwise the time you spend writing postcards could have been spent on a holiday activity. There is no need to provide a blow by blow account of each point of your holiday. Space is limited on a postcard and don't forget that you need room to write the address where you are sending it to. You can avoid using full sentences etc., so a postcard can be written in a short form.

A model postcard

Monday, Aug 6

Hi all, weather great, lovely cottage, can see Lake District, went horseriding yesterday, kids loved it. In Dumfries today, nice town.

Tomorrow going hiking.

Wish you were here.

Genevieve

David Jones
1 High Street
London
W1 1AA

A model informal letter (to a friend or a relative)

1 High Street

London

W1 1AA

1 January 2006

Hi John

Just thought I'd drop you a line to say I'm settling in nicely into our new house. The kids really like their new school and are making friends already, even Georgie is happy here. Will wonders never cease?

The neighbours are smashing, and always willing to help out. I am starting a new job next week as Admin Assistant at a firm of paper suppliers and the staff there are really friendly.

How is Maureen? When is she expecting the baby? Do you know if it's a boy or a girl? I bet Lauren is excited. Send my love to them both.

Lots of love,

Dean

Of course, you are not obligated to use terms like 'Lots of love' if you find them too emotional and unnecessary. We are merely pointing out how informal a letter to a friend or relative can be. You could simply replace 'Lots of love' with 'Take care', 'Regards' or 'Write back soon'. 'Regards' always fits well when you have a neutral relationship with the recipient of the letter.

Conversation

This can be a very challenging area for Aspies. Remembering of course that estimates show that 93% of communication is non-verbal, and only 7% is verbal! For individuals such as Aspies who often struggle with both verbal and especially non-verbal communication this may not be a surprising figure! Naturally conversation relies heavily on aspects of both verbal and non-verbal communication to run smoothly. Many people, even NTs, are not the best conversationalists. Conversation is a skill like any other. It needs to be practised and then honed for it to be a real skill. Some people are naturally great at conversation, some people never will be. As long as you can communicate in a way that you feel is right for you to get by, then how well others manage in conversation is unimportant.

An example of a conversation struggle could be 'getting a word in edgeways'. You might find that you struggle a great degree to get the chance to add your piece to a conversation that is already taking place between at least two other people. Just as frustratingly you may discover that when you finally do manage to make your contribution heard that the conversation has moved on from where it was when you had your contribution in mind. You might be unsure of when to join in, if it is suitable to join in, and what to say when you actually do. This could inevitably lead to either no interaction or unsuccessful interaction.

Conversation tips

Turn taking

One essential thing about conversations is to learn how to take turns. Just as much as you would find it frustrating to not get the chance to say something yourself, think how annoying it would be for others if you were to take over a conversation yourself. Always give other people a chance to join in with the conversation. If someone is fairly quiet, you could ask them at some point if there is anything they would like to add. This makes it less awkward for them and for others in the conversation as they may feel guilty for not having 'let' the quieter person join in. The quieter person may feel better to have been asked directly which takes the pressure off them to interject.

Opening and closing conversations

In any conversation, it is essential to know when it is OK to speak and when to end a conversation. It is helpful to learn how to look for non-verbal cues. For example, if the person you are speaking with is looking away a lot, this might indicate that they are bored with what you are saying or are feeling tired. If the person keeps looking at their watch, this may be because they need to go somewhere, and they are trying to avoid offending you by actually telling you they have to go. Some people do have a habit of being very reserved and hate making a fuss, so might be as subtle as possible rather than be blunt as would perhaps be the case for others. This could be because you keep repeating yourself, which is discussed later in this chapter. However, reading non-verbal cues also relies heavily on the context in which the conversation is taking place. Unfortunately it is not as clear-cut as it might seem.

Eye contact

It is useful to learn how to control your own body language in a conversation as much as possible. As a person with Asperger's syndrome, it is likely that you tend to display some 'inappropriate' or unusual eye contact. In some cases this is making too much eye contact, such as staring. Staring can aggravate people and most people would not find it easy to hold a conversation with someone who was staring or making overemphatic eye contact. Though more common in Aspies is poor or total lack of eye contact. If this is you, you probably tire of people lecturing you or giving you a pep talk on the necessity of making constant eye contact when you are talking to someone, be it in a conversation or just a brief exchange such as when buying something in a shop. We are not about to lecture you or give you a pep talk about eye contact.

The only advice we are going to give is to actually look at the person's face. The closer to the eye the better but if looking at the person's mouth is the closest you can come to making eye contact you are actually doing OK, because in most cases the person will probably think that you are making eye contact anyway.

You could always attempt looking at the person's eyes for brief periods of time but do not worry if you keep losing eye contact with the other person. The person will be happy if you keep looking at their eyes every so often.

Joining in

Also, try to be wary of 'butting in' to other people's conversations. Of course, it will not always be easy to know when you are butting-in and you will need to know when it is appropriate or inappropriate to join other people's conversations. Generally it is inappropriate to join in with the conversation of a group of strangers though there may be certain situations where this is OK. For example, if you are taking a course, and during the tea break a group of people from that course are holding a conversation in the cafeteria you should be fine to join in as they may well have just all met each other for the first time. It should be possible to guess by listening to what they are saying whether they are new acquaintances or a group of friends who already know each other.

Generally, if you know the people in the conversation fairly well it is OK to join in and certainly should be if it is in a private house. In a place such as a public house, this could depend. If the people are speaking quietly and are not interacting with the rest of the pub then you should not enter their conversation. However, if they are speaking loudly and it is difficult to not hear the conversation taking place then it may well be OK to join the conversation, for example, 'Oh yes, I've actually been on holiday there myself.' If you find it too difficult to work out whether your contribution would or would not be welcome, the best advice we can give is to simply say, 'Is this a private conversation or can anyone join in?' Naturally, if it is a private conversation you could feel highly embarrassed by the reaction you receive, but at least they will probably appreciate the fact that you had the good manners to ask.

Do not worry too much if someone reacts unpleasantly to your joining in with a conversation, as it may be that that one person is unpleasant. In fact, there may be nothing wrong with you joining in with the conversation but this person chooses to take exception for some reason. That is not your fault, and it could be that this person is a verbal bully of the type mentioned before who takes great delight in humiliating people and they may have singled you out due to your Asperger's traits. The other people may feel embarrassed by their reaction and may have been more than happy for you to have joined in with the conversation.

Tone of voice

Also, think about your tone of voice. As a person with Asperger's syndrome, you may find it very difficult to avoid speaking in the same tone all the time. However, if you can possibly manage it try to alter your tone now and again according to how you feel about what you are saying. For example, you could speak in a higher pitch to show happiness or enthusiasm about something. If you do not manage to change your pitch, do not worry because many people with Asperger's syndrome lose their monotone voice at some time in early adulthood, which usually comes with increased confidence. If you are already middle-aged, this does not mean that it is too late for you. There is still time to gain confidence and knowing what it is that caused you so many difficulties throughout your life should already give you lots of new confidence.

Also, in a conversation, avoid antisocial habits such as making squealing or whooping noises. Do not speak crudely in polite company. It is more likely that people will think you have a social problem than find you funny and try not to act in a way which people may find creepy, particularly people of the opposite sex. Do not be blunt where this would show you up to be impolite. Do include humour in a conversation where possible, but in polite company, try to be careful – neutral humour is better than very zany or very cruel or crude humour.

Questions

Whatever you do, do not ask too many questions of the other person as this could becoming extremely irritating and they may dread how personal you are going to get. Many people tend not to simply say that they do not want to talk about it. Apparently they would rather try to skirt round the issue some other way and answer in an awkward perhaps slightly flustered way than to tell you that they prefer not to answer that sort of question. Many Aspies find themselves asking many questions on a day-to-day basis as a means of making sense of a somewhat confusing non-autistic world. This is often a good coping strategy, and a helpful means of self-development. However, try to remember, that the world's majority do not question as frequently or repetitively so try to keep this under control.

Interests

As is well known it is not unusual for people with Asperger's syndrome to speak non-stop on just one particular topic of interest! It is good to be so passionate about something, and indeed it may be fascinating for new people to hear you speak about this topic. However, unfortunately, most people will not want to hear about the same topic over and over again, and in a conversation you need to be able to talk about a variety of different things. If you struggle to imagine what other things to talk about, or experience anxiety over what is appropriate and so on, seeking social skills support is helpful. The more you practice, the easier it will become. It is a tough lesson to learn, but no matter how much your interest means to you, and makes you tick, this is simply not the case for most people. Try to limit talking about your interest in great depth to more appropriate situations such as in special interest chat-rooms online, or at groups or forums.

Ending a conversation

All conversations must come to an end at some point and the other person will eventually need to leave the conversation and go somewhere else where they need to be, even if you have all the time in the world, which you probably have not. Whether you or your acquaintance is the dominant speaker you must take the initiative to end the conversation at some point. If you are starting to feel overloaded and stressed, perhaps finding it difficult to keep up a conversation effectively for more than a fairly short period of time, it is best to leave the situation to avoid your stress creating an uncomfortable situation for all involved. You could come across as snappy or appear to lose interest in the conversation, even if that is not really the case. It is best to give at least five minutes warning of your need to leave, so that you do not leave too abruptly. You should, if possible, try to bring the point you are trying to make to some conclusion. If you are pushed for time you could summarise part of what you're trying to explain. If appropriate, you could end with 'and that's what happened'. The best way to take your leave would be to simply say, 'Sorry to cut it short, but I do have to go now. Nice chatting.' Saying this at least five-minutes before you really do have to go will give the other person an opportunity to make some quick closing remarks of his own. You could then leave the conversation by saying, 'We'll have to do this again sometime.'

Listening

You need to learn how to 'listen' to people. For example, someone may want to tell someone about something they are excited about, and it would appear very rude to them if you appear to not be taking any notice. In particular, you certainly need to listen if someone is confiding in you about something or telling you something important. Nothing is worse than talking to someone who is taking no notice.

Try to make eye contact with the person. This could be very difficult at first, and you might find yourself frequently losing eye contact without noticing straight away. The best way to resolve this issue is to look somewhere else on the person's face (the nose if possible but if not the mouth). They will probably still think you are making eye contact anyway and therefore not be quite as frustrated. When listening to people, try to be aware of your body language. As mentioned earlier, you can try just looking at the person's mouth if direct eye contact is too painful. Try also to pay attention to your other actions such as yawning, rubbing eyes, looking at your watch (unless you literally have to be somewhere at a certain time), looking bored, folding your arms or slouching and so on. All these could be interpreted as rudeness by the other person, even if you were not trying to be rude.

It is not useful learning how to take part in a conversation if you are only interested in what you have to say. If you would like people to listen to and take an interest in what you talk to them about, then they would also expect you to extend them the same courtesy by listening when they speak and not interrupting. It may be tempting to finish people's sentences for them if you think you have guessed what they are going to say next, but you should not do this because invariably people tend to find this very frustrating. Just think how frustrated you would feel if you were trying to tell someone something which is important to you, and they interrupted.

Non-verbal 'listening'

Truly 'listening' involves much more than listening literally to the words themselves. If you feel that you genuinely haven't got the gist of what a person is saying because you are struggling to read their non-verbal communication, it is better to ask for clarification. The worst scenario would be to walk away with completely the wrong impression of what a person has communicated simply because you 'read between the lines' all wrong. If it's someone you interact with on a regular basis, asking them to be very straightforward in their communication will be helpful. Whether you explain this in terms of AS or not, you could say, 'I don't pick up on some aspects of communication that well, so I would be grateful if you could communicate with me as bluntly as possible, I won't be offended.'

With people you seldom communicate with, in less important circumstances, don't worry too much whether you have really 'listened'. It is not possible to 'really listen' to everyone you interact with. Prioritise which interactions are most important in terms of really 'getting' the social meaning.

Instructions

In particular, try to listen to instructions. It is OK to ask later for clarification of anything you didn't hear properly but your interlocutor will be frustrated if you ask for clarification on every single point. If you do have difficulty remembering verbal instructions, it may be best if it can be arranged to have the person write them down for you.

There are cases where not listening can mean you do not understand what you are supposed to do when you are in a particular situation. For example, you might have your house to yourself for a week and are given instructions on how to use the dishwasher, turn the heating on and off, water the plants, feed the fish, etc. You need to listen very closely to these instructions. You have to beware of simply agreeing with the person instructing you and thinking, 'Wow, that's quite a handful to take in, I hope I remember.' If the instructions are being given too quickly, ask the person giving the instructions to slow down. Ideally, you would grab a pen and paper and write down all the instructions. Otherwise, you could have a thoroughly miserable and depressing week! Potentially you may not be able to figure out how to start the dishwasher or have to rely on washing the dishes yourself. (Even less fun when there's a machine right next to you that does it, and it actually works!) Another scenario might be that you cannot remember which buttons to press to activate the heating system and so the house is cold the entire time. Or you forget to water the plants and they wilt and worse still it completely slips your mind to feed the fish, at least until you see the house owner's pride and joy floating on the top of the water!

Help or advice

Another reason why you need to listen to people is because they may want you to provide them with help or advice, yet may not necessarily directly ask for it. They might be hoping that you are going to give them advice or provide empathy. Sometimes the person will not want to receive advice but might nevertheless like someone to just talk to about the issue rather than keeping it bottled up. In fact, Aspies often make very good listeners, perhaps partly to compensate for difficulties in being the speaker themselves. In some cases, people will be sharing their emotions with you. For example, they may be upset about something. It may be something that you have done which they are upset about, or it may be nothing related to you and they just want someone to talk to. Often people don't want answers or solutions but just to let out their feelings.

In the case of you having upset them, you certainly need to listen to what they say in order to try and understand what you did that caused them to feel that way. Then you could be ready to justify yourself, and explain that you had not intended to make them feel that way. You may also think about how you would do things differently the next time so that the person does not feel upset or angry on future occasions. If the issue is not related to you, just showing you understand and are genuinely listening is enough, even if you don't really empathise or see their point of view. Don't over-analyse what is being said as often the communication is for the sake of communicating rather than asking for direct strategies.

Auditory understanding

One last reason to listen well is that some people may have accents or styles of speaking which are somewhat difficult to understand, either because the person is foreign to you, has a strong regional accent, has a speech deficiency, is less than articulate or simply speaks too quietly. You may well need to listen intently to the person so that you can hear words, which are very difficult to pick up if you are not paying too much attention. If you do happen to get into a situation where no matter how hard you try you simply cannot work out what the other person is saying then perhaps ask them to write it down. Only do this if it is unavoidable, as this could make the exchange strained or embarrassing for both parties. In most casual conversation you can often get away with appearing to understand even if in reality you haven't by simply smiling and looking as though you understand.

Processing of information

Many Aspies process information in a slightly different way than typical folks. This might be slower, or in another sensory form. A strength many Aspies seem to have is their ability to process visual information better than auditory information. If this is the case for you, try to find a way in which you can process information effectively. Communication is naturally a two-way process, so finding an effective way to process communicated information is essential. It may be that communicating via email is a better choice. This cuts out a lot of issues with slower processing, remembering non-visual information and non-verbal language. Assert yourself in your need to communicate in effective ways for you; try to help others accept that there is not just 'one' way to communicate. Doing this in the first instance may help maintain good communication in the long-term; an investment worth making.

Humour

It is not possible to give a definitive answer for why this is used in social interactions. The most common types of humour used are sarcastic and 'teasing' types of humour, both of which are equally hard to identify and understand in most social interactions. The 'teasing' style of humour is a common one. This might be 'taking the mickey' out of someone, pointing out their weaknesses, behaviours and reactions. This is often not meant literally in the sense of causing deliberate distress but in creating social companionships. How illogical; upsetting someone to create a social bond! Therefore try not to take such humour literally but learn to laugh along and not take it too seriously, rather than launching into a crusade over the cruelness of it.

Learning to laugh at yourself is a handy skill to have since much of this brand of humour is used in everyday interactions. However, beware of people taking 'humour' too far and disguising genuinely unpleasant thoughts under the 'humour umbrella'. It is hard to be sure what is kind and what is not; this too applies to sarcasm. Rather than getting angry or upset, ask others what they think of the humour. If the general consensus is that it is inappropriate, then mention in an emotion-free, assertive way to the perpetrator, 'Do you mind not saying that as it comes across as being a bit nasty. I'm sure you didn't mean it that way, thanks.'

Indeed, much of mainstream humour is based around laughing at social faux-pas, socially unusual behaviour and laughing at the expense of others who are supposed 'social failures'. How tragic therefore that this often seems to be laughing at many of the traits of Asperger's syndrome.

Just as working out other people's use of humour can be a minefield of confusion, so can using humour. Apparently, individuals with Asperger's syndrome have a non-existent or very under-developed sense of humour. Agree with this if you will. Perhaps a more realistic way of looking at it is saying that Aspies often have a sense of humour, but perhaps a less mainstream one. Remember that the mainstream world may perhaps find your sense of humour odd, or at times socially inappropriate. Don't lose your humour just because of this, perhaps just try to minimise who you share it with, as some people will never 'get' it. In some social circles having a 'poor' sense of humour, or enjoying unusual humour, relegates a person to a 'social misfit' instantly, so in these circles it probably isn't worth even trying to help them appreciate a different sense of humour.

Bullying

As we have just said, bullying behaviour is often masked as so-called humour. Bullying sadly continues into adulthood, and often people who are socially more 'naïve', interested in fairness or less socially adapted are the first targets. If you have been bullied in childhood, the outcome can go different ways, causing a person to become aggressive, passive or, ideally, assertive. Assertiveness is the ultimate goal, and often a real deterrent for bullies. The key is to try and understand what motivates bullies and to exhibit as little behaviour as possible that will allow them to achieve their aims. Having AS, and having AS in a society that gives AS a poor profile, means that being assertive might be harder than for the average person. However, don't underestimate your own abilities. One thing that is quite remarkable about many people on the autistic spectrum is the way they just keep on going through all the adversity. Through the lack of support, the lack of awareness, the lack of understanding, the lack of respect: how do people with autism keep on going through it all and still keep getting up, going out, carrying on and achieving so much? It is really quite amazing and deserves so much admiration. Use this strength, this tenacity, this refusal to back down, this wonderful stubbornness to command respect, expect respect and fight for it. There is never, ever an excuse for bullying – don't tolerate it and don't allow it. Nobody, but nobody, deserves to be bullied under ANY circumstances. If you cannot handle it yourself then ask for help.

A selection of sure-fire tips for relating well in any situation

As we have emphasised, so much of communication and relating are not about just what is said, but how it is said and how a person 'comes across'. Whoever said that using non-verbal mechanisms in social exchanges was the right and only way to communicate? This is simply a majority choice, and hence it is not innately disabling but just disabling in a majority context. Get a load of Aspies together and generally communication isn't so disabling. However, using and understanding non-verbal communication is essential to getting by. It would be fair to say that no one, neurologically different or not, expresses themselves or reads others' non-verbal communication perfectly. All non-verbal social communication is a matter of interpretation and up for debate, as it is not factually quantifiable.

Accepting that, as an Aspie, you have to work that bit harder to make up for the different way you communicate and relate is the best starting point. Accept that you will misinterpret others and others will misinterpret you no matter how hard you try but remember that the more you keep trying the easier it will be. Try to educate as many people around you who you think might be open to knowing about AS and autism; the realities and the positives of the spectrum. Try to educate others to 'think outside the box'; remind them that there is more than one way to 'relate' and that the majority way is not necessarily the right way. The more understanding there is, the easier it will be to relate effectively with others. Here are some sure-fire ways to relate positively in any social situation.

Smile

Many Aspies tend to have a different facial expression (from the NT) of their inner feelings. Making others aware of this (either through others or explaining directly) can really aid relating. Some Aspies have one or two facial expressions which represent all of their inner thoughts and feelings. Others have more, but may experience facial ticks and grimaces which may sometimes appear inappropriate in some social situations. One expression which is worth trying to perfect is a genuine smile. As the saying goes, 'a smile costs nothing'. A simple smile goes a long way toward creating good relations with others. However, try to smile from 'the inside' too. This means internally try to think, 'I am here to get on with others, mean to treat others pleasantly and politely and I expect the same in return; I am not a threat and do not perceive others that way.' Feeling this inside may make your smile more genuine. Try practising smiles with people who would give you an honest opinion of how you come across.

Using a person's name

Many people like it if you use their name when interacting with them, it can make people feel really acknowledged and important as a person. It appears that many Aspies can feel uncomfortable doing this, perhaps feeling it is over-familiar or inappropriate. In times when you really want to engage someone, get them to like you or take notice of you, using someone's name can make more of a communicative impact.

Be approachable

This is not about what you say but how you appear. As with smiling it is a tough one for Aspies whose outward appearance often doesn't indicate their inner thoughts or feelings through their non-verbal language (tone of voice, facial expression, body language, implied meanings). However, try practising the following with trusted friends and get feedback over how approachable you appear when you do it: try to soften your body posture. Many Aspies, due to anxiety, look very 'stiff' and 'over formal' so try to soften your posture to look a bit more relaxed. Hard as it is, try to 'open' your body posture so that you don't have your arms folded. It helps to have something to hold to do this, such as a drink, a newspaper or similar. Try to face your body towards others, not away from them.

Body/personal space

This is so important in signalling to others what you think and feel in a social situation. So many Aspies have been in a situation where their misunderstanding of body/personal space has given the wrong signals. This is related a lot with gender. The worst thing of all, it seems, is standing too close to someone, which can seem aggressive or harassing. Standing too far away can look odd, or show a deliberate lack of interest in social relating. Try to observe what others are doing. There is a general unwritten rule about distance that is not definable – have a look around while you are with others to try and work out what it is.

Body language

If you have no idea of how your body language comes across, or are acutely aware that you don't know what to do with your body, try this. If you are unsure what to do, try to observe what others are doing. There are significant gender difference to body language, so try to mirror your own sex, unless of course you have other preferences. It is an idea to copy what others are doing with their body language, but only in a quite subtle way. For example, when you are at a meeting, you naturally fold your arms and look down. This looks defensive and aggressive. You don't feel this way at all. Try to look what others are doing in the majority and try to mirror that.

Eye contact

We will cover this more specifically throughout the guide. However, as a basic rule more eye contact is better than less in most situations.

Show engagement explicitly

Aim to show others explicitly that you are engaging with them. This means that even if in your mind you are interested in what they are saying, you need to make it clear non-verbally if you can. This is done through nodding, use of eye contact and using engaging phrases such as, 'I see that,' 'I didn't know that,' 'Sure,' 'Mmm,' 'Yes,' 'Really?' 'Gosh,' 'Wow.' When someone has finished telling you something, it is often worth reflecting back what they have said such as, 'So, she/he said that, and then … happened, and the outcome was?' or giving a brief summary of what they have said to show that you have engaged with them.

Greetings

Always remember to greet others. The reasons behind this are not as simple as saying, 'Hello,' and, 'Goodbye,' to someone you already know or, 'Nice to meet you,' to someone you don't know. It is about politeness and showing that you are an ally to others. Often Aspies do not see the point of greetings when you already know someone or have said, 'Hi,' once on an occasion. That is a perfectly logical and legitimate thing to think. However, most people do not see it that way. Not acknowledging someone or regularly greeting someone can come across as ignorant, aggressive or rude. Silly it is. Good strategies are when passing someone to smile, say, 'Alright,' 'How's it going,' or making a simple comment such as, 'It's hot/cold/warm,' or, 'Nearly time to go, thank goodness,' or a similar comment relevant to the situation.

Be aware of other's feelings

For some Aspies, asking them to be aware of how others think and feel is as ridiculous as asking them to become a clairvoyant. This is not an innate skill that Aspies have and there are ways to compensate for this, which can help toward relating well with others. One good way is to ask simple questions in a situation such as, 'How did you feel about that?' 'What do you think about it?' 'Are you OK with things?' 'Is that helpful?' Don't go overboard with questions and appear to 'grill' others but the odd question can help you to gain a picture of how people might be feeling about things. If it is someone you interact with regularly, over time you will begin to gain a good picture of how they may react to similar situations.

Think outside of yourself

It is too easy to get caught up with focusing on yourself and forgetting to focus on others. Aspies naturally seem to be more self-directed than others-directed. That doesn't mean that all Aspies are selfish or self-obsessed, it just means that they are wired differently. Therefore in any social situation try to focus outwards onto other people rather than thinking just how you come across, appear and so on. Focusing on others will help you to relax and be less self-conscious and anxious. As an Aspie it is about striking a balance between being self-aware in terms of behaviour but not becoming too self-conscious.

Small talk

So many Aspies struggle with this. Small talk just isn't logical! Why constantly state the obvious:

- 'Ooh, it's raining, gosh look at that rain.' (You're thinking, 'I'm not blind!')

- 'Did you see that goal! What a score for England!' (You're thinking, 'I don't see the point of football or patriotism, so what has that got to do with me?')

- 'How are you?' (You reel off the exact details... they are surprised... did they really care how you feel? If not, why ask then?)

These typical scenarios indicate the different ways of relating for Aspies and NTs. The key is to accept that to fit in to a majority world, adopting some ways of majority communicating is necessary. Try to learn basic small talk rote strategies. NTs often say such obvious things to prove a more general point, such as, 'I am acknowledging your presence as a person,' 'I am not a threat,' 'Just to remind you we are still on good terms.' For Aspies communication is more about relating facts and information. That is fine too, but surprisingly some skills in small talk go a long way to relating well.

Belief in others

If you have had many bad experiences relating to others, naturally you are going to be a bit mistrustful and perhaps appear suspicious or aggressive towards others. If you have been taken advantage of, taken the mickey out of or felt used, why would you want to give others a chance? Sadly, however, the less trusting of people you feel, the harder it is for others to relate to you. The key is understanding that many bad experiences you may have had might have occurred due to misunderstandings by others that you have 'different' but not wrong ways of being in the social world. Hard as it may be, it is worth trying to put basic trust in people from the outset. Some trust and belief in a person's good is the only way to relate positively but some people are never worth investing this effort in. The trick is finding the right people to bother with. Trying to create a network of such people is a good starting point to practice with. Autism specific networks are a good place to start.

Helpfulness

So you may not be the best communicator but that doesn't mean you can't be liked. Showing a genuine interest in being helpful and kind to others goes down well. This might be offering a skill or piece of knowledge that is helpful to others. For example, you are in a job role and want to be seen as friendly but struggle to make appropriate conversation. A good tip here would be to offer to help others out such as making drinks, getting paper for the photocopier or helping others with IT problems. This way you may not gain a reputation for being socially brilliant but helping others shows that you want to create good relations. Try not to get this confused with being 'used' (people taking advantage of what you have to offer giving nothing in return). Be sure not to say 'yes' to everything just to be liked. Being able to say 'no' at times will gain you respect too. Saying 'no' in an assertive way is best. This means add a smile and a, 'Sorry, I can't fit that in/don't know how/… may know,' rather than a blunt, 'No, I can't.'

A note on general safety and vulnerability

It is absolutely essential to take note of this section. Since Asperger's syndrome is a condition that can result in social naivety, never become complacent over your own, or others', safety or vulnerability. Unsafe and vulnerable situations can include getting in contact with the criminal justice system, being abused by others, false accusations and misunderstandings… the list goes on. You could be the most intelligent person in the world, capable of incredible things, yet still be socially 'disabled' or socially 'blind'. There is simply no shame in admitting that social understanding is not your strong point. However, in terms of personal safety, accepting your differences or shortcomings is what will ensure your health and happiness in the long term.

It is too easy to believe that the rest of the world sees things in the socially just, logical and equal way that many Aspies do, and goodness wouldn't it be a better place if they did! Sadly, it isn't and trying to impose these values or expecting others to do the same in the everyday social world does not get results. It is about striking a balance between understanding that the way you see things is not wrong, but to stay safe you must accept that the majority don't see things as you do and this can leave you very vulnerable.

It would be morally wrong and unhelpful for us to try and reel off tips for looking for the signs of a potentially unsafe or risky situation. This is because it is impossible to do so, and is all dependent, as with everything else in the social world, on context. The best advice we can give is to accept your social limitations, forget your pride and denial, and seek support. It is nothing to be ashamed of. We can't tell you exactly where to seek this support, as each individual is different. However, if you feel that you are not getting the right support to keep you and others safe, you have the right to fight for it, and this you MUST do.

Chapter 3

Friendships

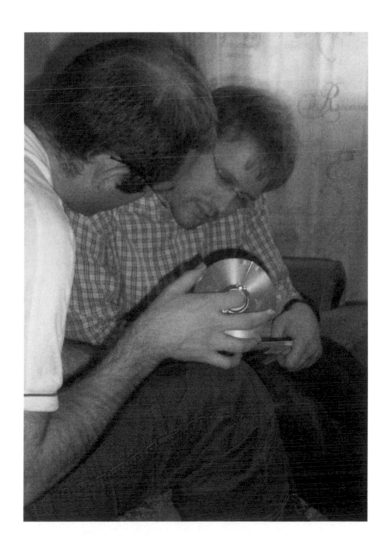

Why have friends and what are they anyway?

This is a ridiculous question if posed to NTs! To some Aspies it may seem more logical. Some Aspies are born less socially motivated than others. Some Aspies desire friends greatly, others continue to prefer their own company. Either one is fine, should the individual be happy with that. However, having friends is certainly good for a person. Friends can bring out all the hassles that having Asperger's syndrome brings, so in the short term it can seem a task too stressful but in the long-term, friends can provide the support or fun that any person, Aspie or otherwise, can benefit from. Friends come in many shapes and forms. This makes the issue of friendship all the more confusing. It would so much easier if friendships came with a rule-book and terms and conditions to refer to! Friends can be 'best', 'good', 'close', casual', 'mutual', 'work', 'family' and so the list goes on. Try not to worry too much about this. Also, try to not to measure your friendships by NT standards. You may choose to have one friend whom you see every once in a while; you may prefer to have more online friends; you may just prefer to spend time with family. It is all about what makes you, as an individual, happy. You have the right to assert your needs, and that you should do.

The key thing to decipher is what you and your potential friend may wish to get out of the friendship. The main criteria a friend should have is that they are 'on your side' (support you), you can trust them, they accept you 'as you are' (faults as well), have your best interests at heart, are willing to share experiences and share some common ground with you. Ideally friends are there to support you, advise you, help you and complement your personality. Naturally it is not as simple as this, but it is a good general concept. A friend is someone who you like to share your life with and they with you (a lot or a little). Friends are allies who are supporting you as you both make your ways through life. You share things together, you help each other out, you go through fun and bad times together. How much friends do this depends on the depth of the friendship. It is important to define this. Friendships go through good and bad patches – sometimes you may not be too keen on each other, or disagree. This is not too important, the key is that you try to stick around and have empathy for each others' needs.

Disclosing AS to friends

This very much depends on the depth of the friendship you are planning to have. If the friend is someone whom you just share activities with, it may not be worth complicating the matter. These kind of friends may not be too interested in how you are socially, but more in the common interests you have, sharing ideas or information. They may not want to know about your mental state or psyche! In this case, disclosing AS may put the friend off, and they may just want to know you as a 'walking buddy', 'drinking buddy' or 'fellow club member' as examples. There is no point in spoiling a friendship by sharing too much information.

If the friend is someone you may have more complex social interactions with, disclosing your AS might be a good idea. This is where having that bit of extra understanding might keep the friendship going. It is all about what you say about your AS. Be aware of the terms you choose to use to describe AS. Terms such as 'mental disorder', 'psychiatric problems' or 'social impairment' might scare some people off! If they have chosen to spend time with you already they may already like you well enough as a person. So in disclosing AS perhaps talk about 'different way of approaching the world', 'a condition like dyslexia, it makes me relate to others differently', 'a thinking style shared by many influential figures, etc.' Using these ideas, it may make disclosure less major or unpleasant in a friendship situation. If problems in the friendship do occur, if you cannot mediate them yourself, speaking to someone who is Asperger's friendly may be able to help give you ideas of how to deal with it.

Meeting friends

Many people meet their friends through activities that they participate in regularly such as school, college, work or social activity. Potential friends are everywhere. Maybe there are people in your college that you sit next to and spend your lunch and breaktimes with and you might feel that this is adequate social contact for you and you prefer spending the rest of your time alone.

You may not like social events although if you can bear it it might be worth going for part of the event as you might get chatting to someone and make good friends with them by finding common ground.

If you don't have an opportunity to go to a social event or you just can't face it, a good way of meeting people who have things in common with you is to join a group related to a hobby or interest. If you're a student, your college or university will probably have something you can join. If you're not a student, in any town or city many groups will exist. The local library or council is a good place to find these places. If you work, perhaps there is someone you work with who can become a friend, but as mentioned before if you work with the person you need to be sure you can trust them not to allow your leisure time to harm your working life.

Creating friendships

It is not as difficult to create friendships as you may think. All it takes is meeting people in situations such as those described above and making a remark or asking a question which you feel the person might respond well to. This could involve small talk such as talking about the weather, but this is something which Aspies often dislike. If you have met through a mutual interest group, you could ask a question which relates to the interest. For example, 'What makes you want to pursue the hobby?' and once they have answered you could explain your own interest.

You could invite the person for a drink in a pub or café or perhaps ask them if they would like to go to a particular hobby shop with you, if that hobby was what brought you into each other's company. Again, get to know the person before you go anywhere private with them. For many Aspies, making friends around a common interest is a good idea. Some friendships, both male and female, revolve around social games, competitiveness and social analysis. The good news for Aspies is that friendships created around a shared interest allow for Asperger's friendly communication, i.e. sharing information rather than social exchanges. Try your best to capitalise on this.

Maintaining friendships

There is a saying that: 'Friends are like plants. If you do not water them, they will wilt away.' Do not rely on your friends to always make contact with you. Keeping friends involves effort just like anything else. If you put the work in, generally you should get a good return. It is your time and effort that you choose to invest, so expecting something back for it is perfectly reasonable. However, try not to be too demanding. It is hard to imagine just what is going through a person's mind/what is happening in their life, so without decent evidence one way or another it is hard to know what can be expected from friends. It is probably an idea to give people the benefit of the doubt initially and broach the subject later. Constant expectations and analysis of the friendship can only serve to cause stress for both parties. Don't forget of course that a friend will have their own friends, and never expect that they will give their all to you, just because that is the way you might feel about them.

Try to make sure that your friendship is as equal as possible. It's about give and take. Your friends ought to be willing to meet you halfway and not want you to do anything that you are not comfortable with. However, you should also be willing to compromise with what they like or dislike doing. If you are inflexible over too many things, you may make your friends feel uncomfortable around you and only a very good friend will stick around, but even they may probably find your inflexibility stressful and find the friendship difficult.

The key is communication. Sending a text, email, online message or quick phone call to catch up is essential every once in a while. How often you do this and to what intensity depends very much on the nature of the friendship. This is something best discussed openly so that misunderstandings do not occur. Again, it's dependent on the nature of the friendship whether you mark important events in the friend's life such as birthdays, Christmas, a new job, engagement and so on. This would usually be done in the form of a card, letter or email.

Tips for maintaining friendships

● Keep up-to-date with their life.

Many friends would be rather pleased if you kept up-to-date with details of what is happening in their life. If you are lucky enough to have a good memory use this as a positive addition to the friendship. Simply asking questions about things they have told you such as, 'How's it going,' 'What happened with the..?' will go down well.

● Focus on 'what makes them tick'.

Most people have things in their life which really 'make them tick'. Focusing on these when you interact should enrich the friendship. You will learn what really 'turns someone on' fairly soon, as most people will bring it up in casual conversation unless of course it is something socially unusual. Simply asking a friend about these things will make them feel like you are in the wavelength even if in reality you are not, it shouldn't matter too much since you are acknowledging them as a person rather than judging their interests or passions. You do not have to be just like someone to be their friend.

● Be aware of how the friendship is developing.

The friendship may be developing into something that one or both friends are unhappy with. The friendship might be becoming too intense or too distant. It is better once in a while to make sure things are going in the right direction. Whether this is brought up directly is an individual choice depending on the closeness of the friendship. If you struggle to take hints or unwritten prompts (to 'read between the lines') it is better to consult someone who may be able to interpret for you who knows the situation.

- Emphasise exchanges of give-and-take.

If a friend has gone out of their way to help you out somehow always try to reciprocate. If you feel that you cannot reciprocate at the time, ensure that they know your appreciation by either saying directly, 'Thank you for... that really meant a lot,' (or similar) or by saying, 'I owe you one' (or similar). Always be trying to think of ways to give and take if you can – this could be very simply mentioning something you heard which may benefit them, cutting something out of a newspaper for them or literally offering to help practically.

- Be a useful complement.

A great way of keeping things going in the friendship is by being a helper in their life. This may be offering to look into something for them or offering skills that you have that they don't. Being a complement to them means that they may be able to offer the same back.

- If it isn't working, try something different.

If things are stagnating in the friendship, don't carry on the same way. Friendships need variety and a change every once in a while.

- Accept that people change or turn out to be different than you thought.

People change, and as such this directly affects the friendship. If someone turns out to be a different person than you thought, don't seek to change them, criticize them or cross-examine them all the time. It is best to accept friends as they are. If you have genuine concerns about the way someone is becoming approach the issue from the point of view of concern rather than judgement. Judgement is a friendship killer.

- Don't forget the basics either!

Don't forget the very basic friendship skills, for example, if they are visiting your house, you need to keep them company. If you leave them in the lounge being ignored by everyone else or feeling that they can not fit in, they are likely to feel uncomfortable and they might feel that you are not a very good friend. Sometimes it is easy to get bogged down with the complicated side of friendships and forget the very basics.

Befrienders, support workers and social groups

Thankfully, such services are beginning to become more common and the more the better. It is sometimes worth looking at social development as a subject to study if you are an Aspie, rather than thinking, 'I am socially disabled; I will not improve.' The great news is that AS is not a static condition and the more work you do on your social development, the easier the social world will become. In terms of friendships, accessing support for your development is also relevant. This could come in the form of befrienders, support workers or attending social groups. These forms of support can provide a bridge for creating friendships and a decent social network should you wish to have one.

Social groups allow for meeting like-minded people (often other Aspies). If you do not wish to associate as much with other Aspies, a befriender or support worker can help to begin to create a social network by offering advice and mediation, or simply going along with you to places where you wish to meet friends.

It is better not to 'turn your nose up' (completely discount something without looking into it) at these support mechanisms. At least try them before discounting them. Many Aspies have a perfectly understandable fear of being seen as 'disabled' or 'mental' by getting involved in these situations. However, you can take as little or as much as you want from them, and if they don't work out the first time, try other avenues.

Online friendships

A number of decent online groups (AS and non-AS) exist on the Internet. This can provide an excellent Asperger friendly way to practise social skills and build up social confidence. That is not to say that some forums aren't picky over social behaviour. It does not mean that just because you may be interacting online that you can do as you please or say what you want! This doesn't go down well online or otherwise. The beauty of online groups is that it makes use of communication styles that many Aspies prefer. Examples are: processing and thinking over what you say before you say it; a log of interactions so you can look back over things you have said that you may have forgotten or wish to check back to, and all importantly, the many advantages of written over verbal communication. Sometimes this written communication can get confusing, but the rather handy use of emoticons (emotional symbols) online enhances written communication wonderfully. The Internet is fast becoming an Aspie haven for socialising. This applies also to online 'chat' services, and messenger services.

IMPORTANT NOTE: Always beware of safety online. The Internet, although mostly a genuine place, does attract (as with any walk of life) unsavoury people, so beware! Don't be overanxious: just follow basic safety rules such as never giving out your personal details, location and contact details unless you are ABSOLUTELY SURE the person you are communicating with is genuine. The beauty of this is that you can use a nickname or username so that you can remain safe and secure. Look on the Internet for more in-depth safety guidelines.

Choosing social isolation

Perhaps due to your personality or the way your AS affects you individually, you may at times choose to isolate yourself from social contacts. This has its own advantages and disadvantages.

Pros

● You find social relating so tiring and stressful that it leaves you exhausted to the detriment of other important things such as work and so on.

● You simply don't enjoy it, so why bother!

● You are having bad experiences with so-called 'friends' who may be abusing you or leaving you vulnerable. In order to break away from them you may need to isolate yourself from them.

● You are going through a bad time emotionally or physically. You know that being around other people when you feel this way can be a negative experience. Taking the time out to sort yourself out away from others might be a better option.

Cons

● You lose touch with the social world, so you may become more eccentric and 'socially odd'.

● Friendships and social relating skills will be lost as they are not being constantly practised.

● Once you have isolated yourself it is harder to 'break back in' to the social world as social conventions change over time.

A selection of social relating strategies with friends

Scenario	Potential outcome	Improvement strategies
Too frequent or infrequent communication.	Friend feels stifled and hassled or ignored.	Avoid emotion when talking about the issue, try not to take things personally. Casually ask whether the level of communication is OK between you.
Narrow interests.	Unless shared to the same intensity friend feels bored and uncomfortable with obsessions.	Explain that you find it hard to know how others feel about things, ask casually if your friend is happy with the way things are or whether you should vary your discussions or activities.
Anxiety, anger or depression.	Frequent meltdowns, panic attacks, inappropriate emotional behaviour, ruins the friendship.	If the friendship is not that close, try to avoid spending time together when you are going through difficult emotional phases. If the friendship is close explain that you suffer from these problems and that your behaviour is not personally aimed at them. Mention constructive things that the friend could do to help when these situations are brewing. Offer to help the friend emotionally too, by saying, 'If you want to talk about anything, I am happy to listen,' or 'Anything I can do to help, please let me know.'

Scenario	Potential outcome	Improvement strategies
Sensory needs.	Friends can only share narrow activities which do not cause sensory distress.	Explain how sensory issues affect you, for example, you may find it hard to go to busy, crowded places or places with strong odours. Assert your needs. This may be a whole new idea to your friend. Try to find mutually comfortable places to go.
Socially unusual behaviour.	Causes the friend to feel ashamed and embarrassed in public, cannot have Aspie friend join in main friendship group.	In this case disclosure of AS is essential. If it is a friend whom you feel you would not wish to disclose AS to, try to avoid situations where you feel your behaviour is less controllable such as when you are tired, tipsy or anxious.
Overtly Aspie behaviours such as stimming.	Can make things very uncomfortable for a person who is very socially ingrained, or narrow-minded.	Explain when and why you stim and ask them to be open-minded about your needs. If they cannot do this, avoid times with the friend where you cannot control your need to stim.

Thoughts on friendships for Aspies

It is ironic, really, that many of the 'issues' that Aspies are supposed to have actually are not always such big issues when they are in the right circumstances, with the right people. Among Aspies can be found incredibly empathic, thoughtful, funny, supportive, kind, caring, genuine, honest people: people who make truly great friends! Perhaps half of the battle in friendships for people with AS is not just the skills alone but finding the right sort of people to be friends with. Perhaps many Aspies find themselves socially isolated not because they are 'bad' friends but because they don't so easily find people who they 'get' and who 'get' them. It seems it is yet another issue of being in a minority and maybe much more energy has to be put into seeking potential friends than for an NT. It might be that in life very few people have the potential to be great friends and that some time will have to be spent searching to find these people.

Chapter 4

Family Relationships

Relating to family

No two families are the same, have the same social expectations, social needs and so on. It is categorically impossible to write this section in a way that will apply to everyone – these are just some general pointers and ideas. For some people this may mean relating to family may be such a hassle that they wish they could have had some choice in who their family were. For others, family are the people in the world that make sense to them and who they find it most easy to relate to.

The thing about family is that there are more emotions flying around to complicate social situations. It is much harder to relate logically and straightforwardly when emotions are complicating issues. The emotional connections (good and bad) with family members often blur simple communication. That does not mean however that relating to family has to be a constant headache. Good communication strategies can be put in place to make relating easier.

Useful communication strategies

Whether you live with family or see them occasionally it might be a good idea to disclose your AS. If you are not happy disclosing your AS, try to explain in a round-about way that you think and behave differently, and assert your right to do this. However, if you can disclose your AS, all the better. Surprisingly, as awareness of autism grows, people are beginning to become more accepting of AS when disclosure occurs, so give it a try. Many families, on discovery of a relative's AS, are often glad to know. Common reactions might be, 'At last, it makes sense,' 'If we'd have known we could have avoided all the problems,' 'Well at least now we can move forward with a better understanding.' The more understanding and information people have about why you are the 'way you are' the less miscommunication will occur and the better the chances will be of relating positively. Here are some common communication/relating issues which can occur in families:

Scenario	How it is perceived	Improvement strategy
Lack of small talk.	Aspie seen as disinterested in family, doesn't care or wish to relate.	Explain that you struggle with 'small talk'. It may not occur to you to 'state the obvious' or ask about the others person. Explain that you do care. Try to find a compromise where you exchange some rote small talk.
Lack of affection.	Aspie seen as uncaring, cold.	Explain that you find some forms of affection hard due to your different sensory make-up. Remind family that hugging and kissing are not the only ways to show you care. Try to compromise with less overt ways of showing affection, such as in writing.
Frequent miscommunication.	Seen as difficult, wilful and uncooperative.	Due to difficulty understanding non-verbal communication, taking language literally and having a rigid thinking style, the Aspie seems to be on a different planet to other family members. Ask family to say bluntly and straightforwardly exactly what they want to get across to you, and what they expect of you.

Scenario	How it is perceived	Improvement strategy
Sensory issues.	Idiosyncratic or senseless reactions to everyday situations.	Explain how sensory issue may affect you as an individual. Examples: sound sensitivity means you struggle to sit at the dinner table as listening to others eating is distressing. Taste or texture sensitivity may mean that you have narrow tastes, which can make family meals a nightmare.
Social/emotional overload.	Seen as emotionally cold and aloof.	Explain that you become quickly overloaded by emotional and social exchanges. Explain that this is not related to how you feel emotionally about others and that you prefer connecting in small bursts to cope with this.
Frequent disagreements over behaviour, outlook.	Seen as socially embarrassing, eccentric or odd.	Remind others that there is not just one way to 'be' in life. Explain that you are an individual, that it is OK not to follow the crowd or the current social trend. Encourage family to be proud of your rare attributes.
Reliance on routines, special interests compulsions and rituals.	Can hold the family back from sharing activities or social freedom.	Remind family that having routines and so on is very important to your wellbeing and happiness, just as some hobbies or more 'socially acceptable' behaviours are to family. Assert your needs and try to compromise between the family.

Relating to parents

The way you relate to your parents is, at times, more important than the way you act with anyone else. The relationship a person has or has had with parents often affects their future social relating albeit in a subconscious way. No matter what the nature of the relationship between you and your parents is, without them you would not exist and therefore having a link to parents is important for many reasons. Avoiding the company of those whom you have a difficult relationship does not usually extend to your family unless they really do, or have done something truly unforgivable. If you do have a bad relationship with your parents, try to do everything in your power to mend this, as your parents are the two people whom you would hope to be able to turn to when you have problems. You might feel very alone if you have nobody to turn to at all. The most reliable way to fix any bad relationships with your parents is to ask for a meeting with them, perhaps somewhere neutral, and ask them directly what went wrong in the relationship and whether there is anything you could do differently to make things better. If it isn't possible to do this face-to-face then write a letter or an email, just don't chicken out altogether.

It could well be some aspect of your Asperger's syndrome that has caused you to have such a difficult relationship with them. If you feel that they would have difficulty believing you, then you could provide them with a leaflet about Asperger's syndrome, and say, 'I have that condition, I'm sure you'll agree that I have many of the traits, and that is why I am so different.' Hopefully, things will then start to fall into place in their minds and they will start to see what it was that was causing the problems. If this does not work then it could be that your parents are being unreasonable out of their own fear, denial or shock.

On becoming adults, very few people leave home and lose all contact with their family. Only people with an extremely volatile relationship with their family might do that. For some people, perhaps who are less socially motivated, keeping in touch may be difficult, perplexing or may simply not occur. Becoming independent when you leave your parents' house and move into your own does not mean that you just say to them, 'It's been nice knowing you,' and not even leaving a contact number. The relationship you have with your parents is ideally for life. When you leave home, give them your new address and telephone number and stay in touch. Some people can go for months on end without any contact with their parents, and this is not unusual, but you should certainly contact them from time to time and mark important events with a card, phone call, letter or email. Do not stick to sending them two cards a year and never phoning or visiting them, and it is an idea to keep them up-to-date with your news, such as new jobs, new partners etc. Above all, don't get married without inviting your parents! Even if you have not been in contact for years, your parents will most likely still wish to see you get married and meet their new son-in-law or daughter-in-law!

Family is not a choice

This means that while it is recommended that you choose friends who will understand and support you, and make you feel good about yourself, you cannot be so choosy about your relatives. Therefore, you need to try get on with them as well as possible and be as supportive of your family as you would like them to be towards you. There are many unwritten social ideas as to why you should stick by family which often make very little sense. You may be fortunate enough to have a social network outside of family who can provide you with emotional support throughout your life but don't push family aside. Many people may not be this lucky, and usually when someone has no one else to turn to they may need to turn to their family, which means being as pleasant as possible towards your family. If you treat family just as you wish because you consider that it is fine to be that way with your relatives whom you didn't choose to have, you may create a distance between you and them, and when you need someone to turn to, your family might not wish to know.

Ways to show appreciation

If you struggle perhaps to show appreciation and love to family through words, or your social behaviour, try and think of alternative means. Alternative means might be something quite unexpected. If you cannot think up these means for yourself try to consult a family member who seems to 'get' social things well, they may be able to advise on what would be good for an individual.

Many families exchange presents, cards and gestures of appreciation. If you receive presents from your family, it would be an idea to buy presents for your family at these times. Even if you see this as unnecessary or illogical it is better not to over-analyse the tradition. Also it is not so much what you buy as the gesture and social meaning behind it. You do not have to get someone a present to thank them for getting you a birthday present, just get them a present for their own birthday. You are not obliged to buy expensive presents if you receive expensive presents, but aim to spend an average amount on each person, whether you really see the point or not.

Tips for relating well with family

Try and seek out family members most similar to you

It is pretty common for Asperger's syndrome, autism or autistic traits to run in families. Usually you will find members of the family, close or otherwise, who will be more 'Aspie friendly' than others. Try to seek out these family members, as they are often the key to providing support for getting along well with family, as they may have experienced the issues themselves or will be able to empathise most efficiently with your experiences.

Try and seek out allies

A family 'ally' is anyone who you can keep on your side, who has empathy with you, whom you have a fair amount in common with and who you would equally aim to support. It is inevitable that there will be personality clashes in any family, so finding an ally is worthwhile. Family members will take sides, club together and have sub-groups within a larger family unit. Your ally could be someone who could advocate on your behalf, help others to see your point of view and for whom you would do the same.

Find a family mentor

If you struggle to understand what is expected of you within the family, or find it hard to work out the social interactions within the family, try to seek a mentor within the family who could discreetly support you socially.

Make family 'friends'

Despite family not being a 'choice', treat family still as friends. Much of the conventions used in friendships still apply to family.

Learn to play the 'family' game

As with other social conventions, many families do not operate on social fairness or logic, so often it is better to just accept that 'playing the game' a bit will get you more of what you want or need out of a family.

Learn the hidden rules

Much of what makes a family tick does not run on explicit rules. Whether you agree with them or not, having an understanding of these unwritten rules can make the difference in creating harmony.

Offer Aspie solutions

Often the alternative views of someone with AS can be very beneficial in social situations. Offering alternative ways of looking at things can often help 'stuck' situations within families. Whilst others without AS struggle with their own inflexible behaviours, an injection of quirkiness or eccentricity can help move social relations in a better or more refreshing direction.

Be proud of your Aspie status

If you have been brave enough to disclose your Aspie status, remember that some family members may not see Asperger's syndrome quite how you might. Ignorance, narrow-mindedness and inflexible thought (apparently the stuff only people with autism exhibit…) will exist among some family members towards difference. Keep reminding them that difference is a good thing, and that you do not require pity, sympathy or patronising (whichever applies to you) as you are just fine as you are.

Educate family in different thinking styles

It could be that disclosure of your AS is not an option, and indeed in some families keeping quiet is not a choice, but a necessity. Family can still be educated in Asperger's syndrome in a less direct way. Talking about different thinking styles with family can be equally as effective.

Getting along in a family household

Housework and house maintenance

Whatever family situation you live in, there will be certain disagreements over household maintenance, levels of cleanliness and so on. Remember that logic does not always determine such matters and some people's attitudes to these issues are not reasonable or particularly rational. Therefore, if a family member places importance on keeping the kitchen clean to the point of obsession, trying to change that by judgement or disagreement may not work.

Emotional and personal space

Remember that everyone differs in their need for emotional and personal space. This might mean practically, in terms of being accused of never 'being' with others, or not leaving others alone when they ask to be. Emotionally this may mean sharing problems together, seeking emotional support from others or sharing feelings. It is very hard to measure out what is acceptable for everyone and stick to it. It is mostly trial and error, and accepting this is better than thinking getting along together has to be perfect all of the time.

Household rhythms

Whatever the family situation, it is inevitable that a household will thrive on 'rhythms'. This will often include allowing for others' routines and need for structure. If your need for routine and structure differs vastly from other household members, serious prioritising needs to be considered. It depends very much on how much you feel you can help your need for structure and routine. It is better to sit down and discuss the issue outright rather than members of the household constantly griping and moaning in an non-constructive way.

Household disasters

Should you have a household disaster for which you were responsible, it may be tempting to hide the evidence as you panic about the consequences, but the person you report the disaster to might be less angry than you anticipated. Most people are calmed with a straightforward, honest and assertive attitude towards whatever has happened than the details of the occurrence itself.

Being helpful

No matter what you do or don't do socially, being helpful is always a winner in a family situation. As with friends, offering skills into a social relationship is excellent. If this is computers, technological excellence, knowledge of cars, the law or whatever, offer your skills to the family. This is rarely interpreted as negative so offer as much as you can. However, don't do this to great excess as people may feel patronised and become irritated if they feel that you are telling them how to do something that they can do perfectly well.

Fussy eating

It is perfectly acceptable to assert your needs in terms of food sensitivities. Not having your needs respected is unacceptable as it can lead to physical and emotional problems. However, this can be a problem if it leads to 'picking at your food' especially around family which they may consider impolite especially if they made the meal. Most people see eating food not as a simple biological requirement, but associate it with many wider social meanings. Therefore, at times, if you can overcome or tolerate some foods, it may be all for the better when there is a social meaning attached to the meal or sharing of the food. It is surprising how over time you can manage to stomach foods that you never could at one time, and there are certainly social benefits to not assuming you dislike something without taking a few bites where possible. Try and put extra effort in with family to accommodate both your needs and theirs by offering to cook and shop separately if required, whilst helping them understand that your needs are acceptable too.

Fussy behaviour

You could cause problems if you are over-pernickety about something, and should try not to correct people too much over minor matters. Indeed, it is certainly an admirable quality to seek detail and perfection in situations but constantly pointing out small issues and being pedantic will achieve nothing with many people, as they will simply 'close their ears to it'. You may point out grammatical errors or be very precise over factual details. They may feel frustrated that you are having a disagreement with them over minute issues that are not worth 'splitting hairs' over, causing unnecessary irritation for everyone and leaving your detail oriented attitude with a negative reputation.

Frustration

Living with Asperger's syndrome is a daily challenge. At times, the tiniest little thing can be very frustrating. You may feel frequently stressed due to your different way of seeing the world and family matters are expected to take precedence. It would be easy to show your frustration by making a scene, debate, losing your temper or swearing at family members. However, trying to maintain calm for a short time rather than completely losing it could mean that the exchange could be over sooner rather than later. Learn anger management strategies, and accept that although you may place less emphasis or importance over some family matters does not mean that there is one right or wrong answer. Try to seek a win-win situation by accepting what others' needs and wants are before judging them by your own.

Good days and bad days

Always take into account that everyone has good and bad days. This might be due to fatigue, illness, disappointment, a bad experience, anything. It shouldn't matter too much whether you understand or not why the person is feeling that way, or whether they should be feeling that way or not. It is not for you to judge one way or another, it is about accepting what people say and accepting that nobody is infallible, so that when you have a bad day you would expect the same understanding.

Deal with grievances in a consistent and constructive way

If there are any concerns, grievances or gripes, rather than disagreeing and falling out, write them down. Any worries or concerns can then be dealt with in a more structured way. Aim to make a time where everyone involved can sit down when emotions have calmed down and compromises can be made more rationally. Making decisions while wound up, irritated or angry gains nothing.

Chapter 5

Work

Is work just about working?

The answer to this is a firm NO. If only being competent at a job itself was enough. Most workplaces keep ticking by not just by hard work but by the social world within them. If you work full time, or even just part time, a large proportion of an average person's life is spent in a workplace. As with relating in any situation it is about 'meeting others halfway'. The present situation for Aspies at work is not good enough. Too few Asperger adults are in employment, and when they are, they find themselves often underemployed or in inappropriate employment for their skills and capabilities. Some of this battle concerns social relating.

Employers and Asperger employees need to be able to compromise on what is really important in the workplace in terms of social relating. Often, what employers think is important is not always as significant as they may think, if they thought a little more 'outside the box'. An example of this might be an excellent employee who produces consistently good results but has perhaps less than 'typical' social relating skills. He may stim inappropriately when stressed and start rocking, he may sometimes forget to observe hygiene rules and he may stand a few inches too close when interacting with others. The boss then sees this as unacceptable, the colleagues are uncomfortable around the Aspie colleague and he ends up disciplined and losing his role, or being redeployed. He comes to work to work and produces the best results, yet more emphasis is placed on less important social issues. If the boss and the AS employee met each other 'halfway', situations like this could be easily remedied. Until we reach that great day when neurological diversity is at last respected, it is an idea to try to conform as much as is needed to get by, as discussed in this chapter.

Disclosure

We would advocate disclosing AS at the earliest possible opportunity with a potential employer. Having an understanding of your AS for colleagues and bosses is essential for effective relating at work. Should there later be an AS related issue in the workplace for which you required support from the employer; you could be disciplined for not having declared AS at the outset. It is fully understandable that many Aspies do not wish to declare AS to an employer for fear of discrimination or being treated as 'disabled', 'less capable' and so on. However, in the 'equal opportunities' world we live in, employment law states that employers have major responsibilities to supporting disabled staff, so in this sense disclosure is preferable.

When applying for jobs, ideally disclosure would occur at interview stage. This would be mentioned on the application form where there is a 'disability' section. Although you may not feel that AS is a true 'disability', in terms of employment, it is classed as such. In this way acknowledging the 'disability' to the employer in a formal sense means that they have a responsibility to meet your needs. When it actually comes to interview stage, this is where you would explain how AS affects you in the job. Just as you would be 'selling' your skills for the job itself to the employer in the interview, you would here also be 'selling' your AS to the employer. 'Selling' in this sense refers to making the employer aware of how the positive aspects of your AS would contribute to the job you would be doing. Then you would talk about the negative aspects of your AS in less detail outlining strategies that could be put in place to make your job easier. On starting a new job, it may be worth discussing the merits of disclosing your AS to colleagues you will be working with. It is understandable if you wanted to keep the knowledge only with your boss, supervisor or Line Manager. However, as we explained, the workplace runs not on ability and skills alone but social relations. In this sense making others aware of why you are the way you are can pay dividends in the long run.

Employment seeking

If you're ringing about possible employment, firstly it's best to ring between 10 and 12pm or 2 and 4pm, as that way you avoid ringing too close to the beginning or end of someone's working day when they might be least helpful, or during their lunch break.

If it is a large organisation, you may have to 'get past the receptionist' so you should ask to speak to the Recruitment manager. If asked the purpose of the call say that it is personal, as some receptionists will actually try to fob you off, for example, by saying, 'All jobs are advertised in the local press,' when this is not necessarily true.

Job interviews

In this section we are just giving basic tips related to AS and interviews. For general interview advice you would need to refer to specific publications and advice services. As with disclosing AS in the job itself, it is also a good idea to disclose AS at interview stage. In the current climate of equal opportunities for disabled people (this includes people with AS and autism) an interviewer has responsibilities to ensure that if a person with AS on application fits the criteria for the job, they must interview them. If they didn't this would be discriminatory practice. Since AS certainly affects social interaction, and communication, and successful interviews rely heavily on effective social relating, declaring your AS at this stage is absolutely worth it. The key is to explain how your AS may affect how you come across at interview. In a sense, it is your disability affecting the interview process, so as such the interviewer must make reasonable adaptations to accommodate your needs.

Try to ensure that, before the interview, the interviewer gets hold of appropriate yet concise information concerning Asperger's syndrome, either by email or post. The best plan is to adapt it to how you are individually affected. Also ensure that you provide a covering letter explaining why you are giving the information prior to the interview. A simple phone call or email would also be acceptable.

Social relating strategies at interview

Eye contact

This would be a particularly good strategy in a job interview scenario for anyone who simply can not maintain uninterrupted eye contact with the interviewer throughout the entire interview process. The good news is that, believe it or not, you are not expected to keep eye contact for 100% of the interview. Many people, particularly Aspies, are unable to make eye contact when they are speaking because it would distract them from articulating their thoughts, but it is much easier to maintain eye contact when listening. Therefore, in a job interview situation, it would be useful to make as much eye contact as possible when listening to the interviewer speak, and then when it is your own turn to speak keep making eye contact with the interviewer every so often. In fact, it is very off-putting for the interviewer if you do not break eye contact during the entire interview. You only need to be making it between two-thirds and three-quarters of the time, and remember the tip about looking at the mouth if it helps. Indeed it will be easier to hear their questions if you are looking at them.

Your social role at interview

Do not try too hard in an interview situation, just try to relax and enjoy the conversation. Always be an equal in the conversation and do not speak to the other people in an authoritative manner. Remember that appearing confident at interview does not mean leading the interview, taking over or lecturing the interviewer. Sometimes Aspies can come across as though they are a bit arrogant, lecturing the interviewer or appearing dominant. Remember, you may have better knowledge, work ethics or enthusiasm for the job you are applying for than even the interviewer him/herself but over-emphasising this is likely to lose you the chance of the job!

Repetition

Beware of repeating what you have said before by just saying it in a different way. It is not unusual for people with Asperger's syndrome to do this. If you have had conversations with the same person in the past, it is possible that they have already heard the same story from you, possibly on one or even several different occasions. You might well wish to convey the story from a different angle. Unfortunately, no matter how fond you are of relating the tale, the person with whom you are having the conversation will probably not wish to listen to the same tale more than once! They may react in a way which you do not find very pleasant or polite, and this can be off-putting for the person with Asperger's syndrome. Having said this, just because the person was perhaps impolite with you when you related the story for the second time, this does not necessarily mean that they will be cross immediately afterwards. They will probably be willing to listen to another story which you have not told them before.

Working as a team

Being a good 'team-player' seems to be a criteria for most jobs. The term 'team player' can make many people with AS feel really put off a job. However, don't be totally put off. Working as part of a team is a skill that can be learnt over time. Some jobs rely heavily on 'team-working' that does not resemble the 'team-working' of others. What will determine how well you work as a team will relate to how complex the 'team-working' rules and expectations are. Basic team-working consists of the following elements.

Helping others out for a common goal

Having a common goal to aim for makes team-working easier . The common goal the team is working for, whether it be a deadline or completing a project provides structure for social relating. It is the job of the manager to put this structure in place. Each team member has an individual role. Your role should be defined by your manager. Sometimes roles become blurred as priorities change such as timescale or content. If your role is becoming blurred, make sure you voice this so everyone is clear. The key is to always remember that whatever the task is, whether you feel it relates to you or not, always show willing to help out or 'muck in'. Being overly pedantic and rigid, saying, 'This is not my job,' is poor team-working. If you feel that you are being 'used' or given the wrong tasks too often take this up in confidence with your manager. Otherwise do not moan or refuse to help out. Often, colleagues will not ask overtly for help initially. If you have trouble 'reading between the lines' about whether you should help, ask colleagues to be clear and blunt about their expectation of you.

Communicating cooperatively with others

Always remember when relating with team members that it is not just what you say, or what you do, but how you go about it. Social niceties, humour and other non-verbal skills are things that you may not be a natural at. However, try your best at these. Often Aspies are perfectionists and can become anxious and irate over difficult situations no matter how small. Trying to learn how to look at things with a neutral sense of humour is very useful. The key is getting a balance between appearing to take things seriously but not being uptight and abrasive. Try to observe how colleagues use humour to deal with difficult situations. The style of humour will differ in different workplaces, so try to work out what is appropriate before attempting it.

Also, beware of how you say things. These non-verbal skills can simply not all be covered in this guide as there are too many scenarios to note! If you struggle to get your point or social meaning across in language, talk this through with a mentor or your boss so that communication is clear all round. Look at alternative strategies to help such as email or in writing or getting an advocate involved. Whatever you do always be grateful to colleagues by using clear statements: 'Thank you,' 'Are you OK with that?' and, 'I appreciated what you did there for me.' This will keep relations clear and cooperative.

Empathy towards other team members

Hopefully your colleagues will have been made aware of your AS, or if not AS, that you may behave differently for a good reason. If you struggle to see others' points of view, try the following. If someone expresses an idea or opinion you disagree strongly with or that concerns you, count to five or ten before stating how you feel about it. Try to think 'around' what they say or do, looking at all angles. For Aspies, seeing things in flexible ways takes time and practice. Accept that this may apply to you. Accept that there may be two or more ways of looking at something. However strongly you may feel, when expressing your opinion try to add, 'I can see your point of view,' or 'I don't fully understand that, can you explain that further?' Even if you can't have empathy, showing you are trying is of equal importance.

Supporting others

There may be some days when members are not performing to their best ability. This happens to everyone, including you. Sometimes the team may lose morale, may be burning out, members may be feeling ill or have personal problems affecting their work. Unless you are the manager, it is not your place to make moral or social judgements about others' behaviour. Keep your thoughts to yourself or discuss them with your manager. If colleagues are not performing well for whatever reason, treat them as you would hope to be treated should you feel the same way. This might mean saying, 'Here, I'll help you finish that,' 'If you're not feeling so good, don't you think you should take a break?' or 'It looks like you're not feeling your best, would it help to have a quick chat?' Whatever you do, show that you are not just 'out for yourself' (thinking only of your own needs).

Listening

At work, it is especially important to listen as there are likely to be repercussions if your boss later asks you about something that you had missed him telling you about earlier. For example, he might have said, 'At 1 o'clock ring Mr Jones and tell him his order is ready.' If you were not listening Mr Jones might ring a week later wondering if his order is ready and you tell him that you do not know and will have to check with the boss. Well, imagine how furious the boss would be if you were to ask him about something he had told you a week ago. Can you blame him? If you have difficulty remembering everything that your boss tells you using verbal instructions then whenever he starts to tell you something which you may have trouble remembering then say to him, 'Can I just write this down please, so I do not forget?' Hopefully, he will wait until you are poised with pen and paper ready to write down his request. If he does not cooperate with this, assert your right to be treated reasonably.

Difficult work relationships

Nearly everyone encounters some difficult relationships at work, but Aspies tend to have more problems in this area than other people do. You may need more frequent support, one-to-one sessions with your boss or outlets for stress and anxiety than most workers. It is best from the outset to ask for help in these areas before problem situations arise. If you are feeling anxious, troubled or stressed never keep it in, as later this could be the difference between keeping and losing your job should you lose your temper or behave inappropriately. Most people will moan openly and air their grievances over other colleagues, company expectations and so on. However, it is often done in a socially sophisticated way which will involve an innate understanding of what to say, how to say it, with whom and when. If you struggle to know these things, it is better to air any grievances in a formal setting only, as it could be used against you by the wrong people, even if you think you can trust them.

Your first port of call would be your mentor or boss. Don't go to other colleagues before your boss as they could give you the wrong advice, and your boss will expect you to see him/her first. If the issue is a big one, you can go confidentially to the Human Resources department yourself to speak to a HR representative or work counsellor. Keep this to yourself and don't inform others what you are doing except your boss. If the issue is with the boss him/herself, seek advice from HR only from the outset.

As an Aspie you are best to keep your head down and get on with your work. Of course, we're not suggesting that you don't chat with your colleagues at all, as that would send out the impression that you're hiding something, but you're best to stay reasonably quiet. That way you avoid as best you can any situations which may cause you problems. For example, even if it makes you look boring you're best to keep your sense of humour largely to yourself and not give opinions or talk about anything personal. You might think it sounds over the top telling you to keep your work life and private life so separate but it will reduce problems that could potentially arise. This might sound hard, but it saves you from being implicated into anything awkward. For example, when you start work someone might ask what you think of the boss. The boss will probably eventually find out what your reply was, so don't give an opinion that will get you on the wrong side of your boss. At the same time, it might be as well to say you'll reserve judgement seeing as you're new, as saying the boss is OK might not go down too well with your colleagues.

Out of work socialising

In many workplaces spending time outside of work with colleagues is common. Naturally, people who may be straightforward to relate to in the workplace become all the more complex outside of the workplace. Socialising, in its purest sense, with colleagues allows for a more unstructured environment. The less structured the environment, the more confusing it gets. In some work sectors there is an unwritten rule which states that socialising outside of work time is expected. Hopefully you might not work in these sectors! Other sectors place a fair degree of emphasis on socialising while others none at all. If you choose to not socialise, the key is how you turn down invitations and how this then affects relations with your colleagues.

In the workplaces where socialising is common, much of the office chit chat may revolve around what happened when everyone last went out and associated gossip. If you continually refuse to go along on such occasions, it could make relationships potentially difficult with these colleagues. You may feel like you are constantly having to lie.

If you do decide to go out socially with your colleagues aim not to drink too much as if you get too animated, you might make a fool of yourself which could cause you problems at work as you won't be taken seriously.

Hierarchies

Workplaces have hierarchies and the higher up the hierarchy a colleague is, the more thought you need to give to the way you interact with them.

Around managers you need to act very responsibly. Do not natter when a manager is about. You should at least try to look as if you are working hard and you should act responsibly, even if not serious, every minute. By this we mean you can smile and perhaps even laugh politely if the manager says something mildly humorous, but you still need to be seen to be taking your job seriously. Managers are busy people, so it's probably best not to have a conversation with them unless they initiate it. However, if they are walking past you should at least look up and say, 'Hello,' and then look down again and continue with your work. In some larger companies it is not policy to call managers by their first name and you need to address them as, 'Mr Smith' etc. However, this practice is a lot less common than it once was and you may well be allowed to address all managers by their first names. In which case, using their formal titles would seem pompous.

Even in companies where senior management are addressed with formal titles, it is usually acceptable to address supervisors by their first name. It will soon become clear when you start work how you may address them. You'll no doubt have a more informal working relationship with your supervisors than you will with your managers, and they can sometimes seem like your friends and you can perhaps have a bit of a laugh with them. However, they do have to report back to the managers about your performance so you can't afford to let your guard down too much. You still need to get on with your work and though it's fine to have a little bit of a laugh and a chat, you still need to appear sensible. Don't become the department joker, because no one will take you seriously any more as an employee.

Also, don't get complacent with your same-level colleagues. Again, you can chat and maybe laugh at one or two of their jokes, and even go out for the occasional drink with them. However, if you want to be sure to be taken seriously at work, you can't afford to let your hair down too much. In this case don't get too drunk at the office party and don't give away too much about yourself that might be seen badly or humorously. Keep your work and private life separate, particularly if you wish to pursue development opportunities. Also, avoid gossip about other people as it could get you into trouble, particularly if you're asked your opinion on the boss. It is best to keep opinions to yourself.

Office politics

Many companies, even in non-profit making organisations, have 'office politics'. The best course of action for dealing with this is to perhaps try comparing them to Government politics on a vastly reduced scale. You know that no matter which political party you follow that someone else will be fiercely opposed to your views. In work, it works the same way. The best way to avoid being at conflict with the colleagues who take the opposing view to your own is to take the same way out as people who are confused by all the different policies of politicians – they simply don't vote. Just as someone might avoid disagreements outside of work by not following government politics, you could take the stand of not following office politics, regardless whether you vote in political elections.

The best way to get by at work is to make yourself impartial. It is not advisable to take sides with colleagues with regards to workplace issues, because this can cause disputes. In a lot of workplaces there are divisions between the staff even within a department. If you get involved in differences between staff you could make yourself unpopular with some of your colleagues and this could make your life at work difficult. It can get very complicated and you should avoid, if possible, becoming embroiled in such a situation. The best way forward is to just go there to do your work, get paid and go home. If you can get involved in formal committees, action groups, unions and so on, this is the best place to get involved in Office Politics without risking your job or credibility. Indeed, as a general rule, it's OK to have neutral conversations with colleagues but it's not worth giving strong or controversial opinions about colleagues or any issues that are going on at work.

Sensory needs

How well you relate with others at work could be affected by your sensory needs. Most Aspies one way or another don't perform well socially when they are overloaded. Many workplaces, unless you are lucky enough to have your own office or work in near isolation, tend to have many sensory stimuli. It is perfectly reasonable to ask your boss if you can work in a less sensory environment. The key would be to explain that when there are too many sensory stimuli, it is much harder for you to communicate productively. You need to pitch this issue clearly to a boss who quite likely does not experience sensory overload like you do. Therefore, when you first mention it, the issue may make no sense at all to your boss. If you feel you couldn't get the point across, ask for help with this, such as getting someone to advocate for you, or by emailing useful reading material for your boss to read to understand the issues more clearly. The best idea is to ask for what you want in a way that makes it seem worthwhile to your boss.

Scenario	How it appears	Strategy
People chatting while Aspie is trying to concentrate.	Person is rude and unsociable.	Ask colleagues to chat to you only at break times as this can be exhausting and mean that attention-focus shifting is hard for you.
Stims whilst working.	Unnecessary, 'oddball' behaviour.	Try to stim in more 'socially acceptable' ways, ask for space to be alone to 'unwind'.
Office lighting is bright, desks are close together.	Employee gets ratty and stressed easily.	Try to ask for sensory-friendly space to work whether this be in a side-room where sensory input can be controlled or in a sectioned off area.
Concentration goes in 'waves.'	The employee is lazy and unfocused.	Remind boss that constant sensory input means that you can 'zone out' to deal with it, meaning that you need frequent breaks away from sensory input to 'refocus'.

Social games

Another thing which colleagues do is play games with each other. As the new recruit, someone might try to see how far they can push things with you. Also, beware of people who have no supervisory position but try to make you do things for them. They might be trying to see how far they can push you. If you have any doubts whether the supervisor has asked this person to delegate duties to you, then ask the supervisor about this. It is possible that in some cases, the supervisor will ask your colleagues to delegate work, but they might not have said whom to delegate to. Of course, if you refuse these requests every time, you could end up with no work to do, but if you accept each time, you could be overloaded. Make sure that you don't become like everybody's slave. Do your fair share, but do not do more than your fair share unless you can cope with it.

Quick tips for relating well at work

- Say 'Hello' and 'Goodbye' to your colleagues each day and engage in some chat. A few 'chatty' comments per hour should suffice, such as, 'What did you do at the weekend?' 'What do you think of the new system?' 'How did... (person's important event they told you about) go?'

- Treat managers with respect and be friendly and approachable with colleagues and supervisors.

- Let someone know if you're having difficulty and ask for extra training if you need it.

- Be willing to help staff where needed.

- If you feel its appropriate ask if someone can be your mentor. Having a mentor could be your saving grace as they could be your 'social interpreter' which could just save your job.

- Offer to make tea or coffee now and again, even if you don't drink it. It's not the act itself that counts, but the meaning behind it, i.e. 'I'm acknowledging you other workers as human beings.'

- Get your head down and get on with your work, even if others don't. Don't be fooled by others who mess about yet never seem to get in trouble. Sadly the workplace does not operate on an equally and socially just basis. Some clowns are good at 'playing the game' and get away with anything with the boss, but as an Aspie don't try. It is better to gain a reputation for being a hard worker than a poor 'social game player'.

Quick tips: what not to do when relating in the workplace

- Don't address managers by their first name if the practice is to use their title, and vice-versa. If they specifically say, 'Call me Bob/Linda/Sue/John,' use that name.

- Don't get too familiar with managers, and don't show them disrespect. It is fine to make some neutral chit-chat with them, but leave any debatable or controversial topics.

- Don't swear around managers and don't be argumentative with anyone. Whilst it might be OK for managers to swear and become argumentative, that is a privilege they have for being higher up the 'hierarchy'.

- Don't let people use you.

- Don't give colleagues any opportunities to not take you seriously.

- While you should chat a little, don't gossip about others or talk about your personal life. The gossip game is a complex one. When someone shares gossip with you, rather than saying, 'I don't gossip,' or, 'Gossiping is cruel,' just retort with neutral comments such as, 'Really?' 'Gosh!' or, 'I didn't know that.' Don't elaborate on these. If someone forces an opinion out of you just say, 'I don't know that person's circumstances well enough to comment.' That should shut them up.

- Don't attempt to be the office entertainer. You may be a witty, funny person to your own friends but often Aspie humour doesn't go down well with the mainstream.

- While you might come out looking quiet and boring, that is the problem of your colleagues and not your own. Better to have a reputation for this than anything else.

- In fact, keeping your head down could impress your bosses. After all, as Aspie logic states, you are there to work! (Why is that so often forgotten by NTs?!)

Chapter 6

Relating at University

Relating at university

Ideally universities should be a haven for Aspies. What could be better for an Aspie than spending all their time obsessing over a favourite subject in an academic setting? Sadly, many universities have gravitated to becoming businesses and hence are becoming overrun by people not really in it for the pleasure of studying a subject, but committing that horrendous crime, 'I want the degree, I don't care about the subject.' In the majority of universities there seems to be more emphasis placed on the social world than your degree! Due to this, a seemingly Asperger's-friendly environment can turn into anything but. Starting university can be a very traumatic experience for Aspies, but many Aspies have faced the fear and managed it anyway. The social scene on your university course will doubtless be very different from how it was at college, school or work. This could come as an unwelcome shock, so be prepared.

Open day

Your first opportunity to relate to people who might be on your course and tutors who might teach you is at the Open Day. You are likely to attend Open Days at more than one university as you are unlikely to be 100% sure which course you will study and where. If you are quite impressed by any of the universities you are visiting, then it would be helpful to make conversation (if you dare) with other people there. Of course, some Aspies may find it much too uncomfortable to approach more than a few people, but the more people you approach, the greater the possibility that when you start university you already know someone. Ideally, aim to approach three people at the open day as that is not so daunting. It would be very easy to not dare to speak to anyone but do not forget that everyone there is in the same boat and each individual is nervous, which means you have nothing to lose by saying a few words to someone. Do not bombard anyone with questions but try the following suggestions:

What do you think of it?

Have you come far today?

Do you think you might come here or do you like somewhere else better?

It might be a good tactic to speak longest to the person who seems to be the keenest of the three on that particular university. At this very moment, you might be thinking, 'There's no way I can do that!' OK, we are aware that there are some individuals with crippling shyness who might go through their entire university career only ever speaking if spoken to, but it is untrue that the vast majority of Aspies are shy people. The reality is that they find social situations more confusing than other people and are not quite sure how to make the first move. Yet when they do so and persevere when they do not always get it right at first they can surprise themselves at how well they do get on in a social situation. They possibly won't ever be as outgoing as their peers, but will at least try and this is enough!

If you chatted to someone at the Open Day, this might ease the path to approaching that person in your first week of the course. A good strategy would be that on your first day, you look out for faces from the Open Day whom appear to be on their own. If you are the first person to approach them, you might become their best friend on the course.

Admissions tutor/interviewer

In many cases this will be the same person and in other cases no interview is required. You will need to interact in the same manner with both the Admissions Tutor and the Interviewer, though some students will need to meet neither one to be accepted onto the course. If you have to prove a particular skill at your interview such as speak a language, this will probably only be for a few minutes. It may be that proof of that skill will be enough for you to get onto the course, and therefore there is nothing to fear. You need to be honest with the Admissions Tutor or Interviewer about what sort of grades you expect to gain, as you might be able to negotiate a little. For instance, if you are doing a vocational course and they ask for a particular minimum grade in certain modules. If these are your weakest modules, then say something because they might say that you can still take the course if you make up for it in other modules. Wherever weakness exists, you must always add at the end, '…but I make up for it by…'

However, do not mention weaknesses if there is no necessity. For entry to some university courses, showing a good personality at the interview can help, particularly if you do not quite get the grades you expected. Sometimes, even with the right grades, you can be turned down for being considered too quiet at the interview. Do not be disheartened if you attend a university interview and do not manage to hide your quieter side. You might still be accepted, particularly if you get the right grades, but as we say in some cases, ridiculous as it may sound, you will be required to be a bit of an actor or actress. You may be surprised at how well you are able to keep up the act. Just try to think of the interviewers as friends, while not resorting to inappropriate behaviour such as swearing.

Freshers' week

The first week of the year for new students could end up putting some Aspies off university for life! That could be a wild generalisation, as some Aspies may relish the sensory overload, the illogical behaviour, the horrendous volume of social interaction, the humiliation and so on... each to their own! Freshers' week does not have to be a negative experience if you handle it in a clever way. Freshers' week only becomes intrusive and unpleasant if you let it! Each university differs but emphasis is placed on much lengthy unstructured social interaction under the influence of alcohol and so on... If you happen to be living in shared university accommodation, your room-mates will expect that you will join in, and if not you may be seen as 'odd' and your so-called 'socially isolating behaviour' may cause concern among staff and students. This will be the week when people will mix most, form friendships, make acquaintances, and begin forming a social reputation. If you feel this would be too much for you, it is best discussing the possible issue with your student support network beforehand, so you don't end up getting highly anxious in your first week of university.

Clubs or societies

As an Aspie at university, join a club or society if at all possible. Of course, many Aspies are loners and will wish to limit the amount of time spent on social contact. In many universities, clubs and societies meet on a Wednesday afternoon. Of course, you might feel that you would like to use that time to be alone. However, it is imperative to meet as many different people as possible when you go to university, as unless your family live nearby or you go home at weekends, you could do with having someone to talk to when you feel bored.

When you start your course, you will be unable to predict how well your social relationships with other students will turn out. It is for this reason that we recommend that you invest your time in as many different social situations as possible when you first begin your course, even if initially you are the wallflower who sits in the corner for two hours before someone finally speaks to you. This is not to suggest that you spend the entire year being some sort of social animal. It is just to suggest that you start off with more than one set of friends so that if one group starts to keep their distance, you still have other friends to spend time with. For example, you might join a club then stop going because you have made friends on your course that you'd rather spend your Wednesday afternoon with.

Something that you can't put your finger on makes these friends gradually less friendly with you and they no longer seem to want you around. You return to the club, but everyone seems to have bonded and again you feel left out.

Therefore, it would be best to remain a member of the club so that if one friendship group became distant from you, there is still another one to fall back on. The other good thing about being a member of a club is that if any friendships you make there do falter then there is bound to be someone else there that will be nice to you. Even if you make no firm friendships either on your course or in the club you've joined, it will still be worth going along on the Wednesday afternoons for the company. Even if you spend 90% of the time not talking, it is highly unlikely that you will be completely ignored by every single person. Also, if there is no social life on your course itself, being a member of a club would be a good way of having social contact, even if you rarely say more than, 'Hello.' On a university course, it is not unusual for someone to sit next to the same person for four years and never speak to them.

Halls of residence

This would not be suitable for all Aspies, but most people on your course will probably make friends at Halls of Residence before you even take your first lecture, which leaves students not in Halls at a distinct disadvantage. Of course, as an Aspie you will have an even greater setback in terms of getting to know people on your course if you are not in Halls, so it may be worth casting aside any reservations you have about living there. OK, so you might not take kindly to being the mug who has to answer the door at 3am now and again to some drunken students who forgot the security code but if you don't live in Halls, you may end up having to be creative at making friends and maybe even go outside your comfort zone.

There can be some lively characters in Halls, and not everyone will study all the time. You may also get some cases where people are taking illegal drugs. This certainly does not mean that you are obliged to take them yourself. If you don't approve then simply avoid the company of the people who take them regularly. If you are offered drugs then its fine to politely refuse.

House mixing days

If your university or a local organisation organises house mixing days, these are a useful way of meeting potential housemates if you are not moving into halls. Some may be organised by theme, for example, business studies, gay students, so it would help if there was a theme which suits you. The theme most likely to suit students with Asperger's syndrome or other Autistic Spectrum Disorders is Disabled Students. Although we dispute whether AS is a disability ourselves there could well be another Aspie there, and this could be ideal for you. Naturally you won't be compatible with every Aspie you ever meet, but you are more likely to find someone on your wavelength among other Aspies. If there are no themes then just go along to a general mixing day. It would help if you introduce yourself to one or two people, perhaps those standing or sitting closest to you. You do not need to shake hands unless they put out theirs although even if shaking hands is not your natural style, it can actually be a useful technique for hiding a lack of confidence, particularly if your eye contact is poor.

Private accommodation

Before you meet the people you will be sharing with, you will probably meet your landlord. Don't be intimidated by this title. You only need worry about being on the wrong side of them if you abuse your tenancy, although having said that, there are a number of unfair landlords who don't treat their tenants well. A good landlord will leave you alone, as long as you treat his property with respect. Causing minor damage is unlikely to cause you to be evicted unless you have an extremely unfair landlord. Do be aware of potential problem landlords. If you have a bad experience with a landlord, don't sit back and say nothing but reason with him or her firmly but fairly. Do not resort to aggression as you may be evicted.

You might prefer to live in a shared house or flat, usually with other students though if possible you might prefer sharing with young professionals. If you share with young professionals, they will usually be in bed by midnight and cause you less disruption than will possibly be the case if you are sharing with other students. It will help if you are able to meet your fellow housemates before deciding if you want to share accommodation with them. You might have the opportunity to share with other people from your course. Find out in advance if your university runs 'mixing days' which may be divided up by subject area.

Living with other students is invariably not a civilised experience: for example, many students are very messy. You may find yourself clearing up a lot after your fellow housemates, but do try to persuade them to do their fair share – be firm but fair with them. Do not allow yourself to end up paying more than your fair share of the household bills. Apart from paying for the Television Licence if the television belongs to you, you should not have your name on more than one bill, as otherwise the others may take advantage of your better nature. Do not allow your housemates to bully you into anything, although obviously do your fair share of household chores and pay your fair share towards household bills. Just don't allow anyone else to get a free ride. If you have the opportunity to go to the pub with your housemates, then do go along as this might well provide your only social outlet for the rest of the year. Having said that, don't rely on your housemates becoming your best friends for the year.

Your course

As suggested above, your relationship with coursemates may depend largely on whether you know them already by living in Halls or private accommodation with them. If the other people in your house or flat are doing the same course as yourself, they won't necessarily be in any of the same groups, and even if they are, there is no guarantee that you will get along with each other. If you arrive on the first day meeting having never met another soul from the course, then you will have your work cut out. It is no use assuming that someone will eventually speak to you. Some people not in Halls will have met other students at the open day which took place when you were working out which course to choose, so if possible pluck up the courage to speak to the people at your Open Day so that you might have a head start on your first day.

You should really make a concerted effort to speak to other people on your course after lectures, for example, in the corridor or canteen. If you sit down at the same table as your coursemates, do make sure you speak to them. If you're relying on them to break the ice, they might just be wondering who you are and why you are sitting at their table but not actually asking you, and you will most likely feel very strange. It is certainly nerve-wracking to actually manage to say something, but what you need to be aware of is that you might rarely ever be spoken to by anyone on your course unless you make the first move at some point. You could find yourself wandering around entirely alone for the first couple of weeks until you finally pluck up the courage to speak to someone. Having said that, if ultimately you do not find the courage and indeed you have no social contact on your course whatsoever, it is likely that you will eventually be required to do groupwork. The others in your assigned group will be need to speak to you at this point.

Relating in lectures and seminars

Specific social rules apply when in seminars/tutorials and lectures. Different universities have different expectations and levels of formality in these conventions. If you can't work these out for yourself it is better to ask more explicitly to save any embarrassing situations.

In lectures, unless you are invited to ask questions or interject with comments, don't. Every lecturer differs, so observe others to get the idea. If you are unsure, ask the lecturer directly what is acceptable. If you really struggle sitting in close proximity to others, with large numbers of people, it is acceptable to ask for a notetaker or to record lectures.

There is much emphasis placed on group learning situations at university. This can include seminar groups, study groups and group presentation exercises. It could well be that you learn best as an individual or in a small group/one-to-one setting. It is highly discriminatory to enforce group learning styles on a student if they don't learn that way, and you must assert your right to learn in a different, not 'wrong' way. Group learning situations require an understanding of many unwritten social rules; the ability to cooperate with others and to take on a variety of roles. If you find that you are spending more mental energy on trying to work out how best to interact with other students to the detriment of your learning, then you need to ask for help and alternative means of learning. All too commonly, AS students miss out in learning situations just because they don't 'fit the mould' of the majority. This is simply not acceptable, and don't be victim to this.

Dealing with administration

When you enter your accommodation share, you may need to contact utility authorities that you pay bills to, e.g. the gas board, electricity company and council tax department. This is so that they know that someone is living in the property. If you do so, you will be asked a series of standard questions but this is not too hard. It may be best to wait until everyone has moved in and the contract has been signed before you contact the utility companies. Be sure to ask other students' permission before you add their details onto official forms, as some students might have reservations about doing so, which is their problem not yours. Organisations do make mistakes, and in some universities you will be the victim of administrative errors and perhaps told that you might have your degree withheld for not paying for something that you actually did pay for. In such a case, simply go calmly to the relevant office and explain what has happened. More often than not, they will resolve the situation before you leave the office. Relating to others successfully in a student house seems similar in a lot of ways to those discussed in the 'family' section.

Support networks

In some universities or university cities you will be able to gain access to either a university-based support worker who can help and advise you with relating to other students as well as other things. However, this might merely contain two hours weekly of talking through things you found difficult and ways to overcome obstacles. For more hands-on help, access to a befriender may be available, although their role tends to be to accompany you to places you wish to go. For example, they might go along with you to the student union bar one night a week and play pool with you, and perhaps they will assist you in forming social relationships with other students who are at the bar. It will be a bonus if any of the students in question are on your course.

Perhaps in a few cases the university can arrange for one or two of your classmates to help you to integrate a little, perhaps without AS even needing to be mentioned. The remaining support network that will perhaps be available is the local Asperger's group, if one exists. Also there are some websites for students with Asperger's syndrome, just key in 'Asperger's syndrome + student' into any good Internet search engine. Through these you can learn about other students with Asperger's syndrome and perhaps even write with them or possibly eventually meet each other.

As already discussed in Chapter 3: Friendships, asking for help and making use of services such as befrienders may feel like a step back in social development. However, accepting you might need help to develop is never going to be a negative step.

Relating to lecturers and tutors

At university, there is a completely different style of tutor-student relationships to in a school, or in a workplace. With the possible exception of a few, it is a fairly informal relationship. It is rare to call a university tutor Sir or Miss, and in the majority of cases, you will be on first name terms with them, and there are even instances where tutors will have a drink with students at a social event. However, professional boundaries do still exist and lecturers are technically not permitted to have romantic liaisons or close relationships with their students. You should show your lecturers respect as they are helping you to get a degree or another type of university diploma and it would be unwise to annoy someone who is giving you a grade that may go towards your final qualification.

At university, not all lectures are compulsory, though some tutors will summon students who miss a lot of the same module, especially tutorials or seminars. Some tutors do show annoyance at late students, but in most cases being late at university is not the end of the world. However, aim to be on time and if you miss the occasional class or seminar your lecturer will probably not mind, though it would be more acceptable to email or telephone to let them know that you will be ill or give an adequate reason for non-attendance. This is not recommending that you adopt a laid-back attitude and start to struggle with your coursework. It is best to be clear what the individual university expects as this varies widely.

Relating to students at large

By students at large, this means students who you generally encounter around campus whom you were not planning to meet, for example, someone that you have an encounter with in the grounds, in the library or in the Student Union building. It is fine to approach other students that may happen to be in the vicinity, for instance, to ask for directions to a lecture theatre or whether they can change some coins for the phone. Don't be too familiar because there are no 100% guarantees of whether a stranger is safe or not, student or otherwise. Do not carry out any big favours for someone you do not know such as lending money, as you will probably not ever get it back, and besides you should not lend money to anyone unless they have proven their trustworthiness. In the Student Union bar, it is fine to have a game of pool with a student that you do not know, but be wary of playing for money, or engaging in any gambling activity with other students, for example, cards.

Chapter 7

Relating to People in Specific Situations

In the following section there are several different social scenarios in which the way that people relate to each other will vary and you will be expected to follow suit. General unwritten rules apply and we have noted a very brief selection of these. Don't try to find logic in them as there isn't much! Some people who break these unwritten rules are strongly penalised; yet other people get away with breaking the rules with no problems! Don't try to rationalise this. Again, as we have stated previously, a strong sense of social justice and equality is a quality often found among Aspies. However, in the general population there are often less people with this quality.

NB. Don't take these suggestions as hard and fast rules, as they are not. They are merely a light-hearted starting point from which to think about the unwritten social rules in specific social situations. Otherwise they wouldn't be unwritten social rules which are formally unregulated, and we would not be writing this section!

Strangers

Naturally, it's OK to speak to strangers as a general rule. Whatever you do, do not get into a private vehicle or go into an enclosed private building with someone you do not feel comfortable with. If you cannot trust your personal instincts, don't take a chance. Do not provide strangers with your personal details (other than strangers doing their jobs with appropriate identification personal details). Also, always think twice before telling strangers that you have Asperger's Syndrome. It is not helpful to tell every person that you have an encounter with.

Be wary of strangers approaching you in the street. Very often they are asking for money. Some of them are quite clever. The easiest way to avoid parting with money is to ignore the person. The best thing to do is avoid eye contact and walk purposefully past. If they accost you, be firm yet polite and say, 'No thank you,' and leave it at that. However, this could cause aggression from some people, so you would be better if you feel confident doing so, to politely telling them, 'I have none, sorry.'

Also, beware of people with clipboards or people trying to sell you anything. Quite often money is not mentioned until several minutes into the encounter and it can feel awkward to back away. The best policy is to just say, 'Sorry, no thank you.' If they try to bring the price down then you may have no option but to say, 'Sorry, I'm not interested.' The best way to avoid these situations is to either ignore such people altogether or just say ,'Sorry I'm busy,' depending which you are most comfortable with. In particular do not answer any questions which give away what goods are at home, because if you give your address for correspondence, you could go home to find it burgled if no one was in.

Age groups

The way you speak to people tends to depend on what age group they are in. Aim to treat all people with equal respect regardless of their age, though aim perhaps to pay more care to children and older people. When speaking to young children try to moderate your tone to ensure they understand you, but don't talk to children over the age of three as though they are still babies. Just speak to them clearly and gently.

When speaking to people over the age of thirty you would usually make more of an effort to be polite and respectful than you might if you were speaking to someone under thirty. That's not to say you should be impolite and disrespectful towards people under thirty, but you can afford to be a little less 'serious' or formal. However, don't overdo it, as no one will then take you seriously.

When speaking to anyone over seventy, perhaps speak more loudly as they are more likely to have difficulty with their hearing. Keeping things neutral is also probably best with the older generation since naturally generation gaps will cause conflict. 'Always respect your elders' as they quite possibly have more experience of life than you have, which should really be respected. If you are talking to someone elderly they may delight in taking about the way life used to be when they were younger and maybe the war, for example. Often the younger generation seems to moan about this, '… on about the war again (sigh).' Try to listen intently to them and do not underestimate any part they may have taken in past major events, and avoid making any strongly opinionated inappropriate comments that may offend them.

Whatever age group you are interacting with, the best thing to do is remove any stereotypical ideas about anyone you meet just by looking at them, that way showing an open-mind will create a bridge of understanding and empathy even if you do feel 'socially blind' as to what to do.

Backgrounds

Also be aware of different backgrounds, aim to treat people of all backgrounds equally. This is quite helpful for Aspies, since many Aspies do this anyway, as differentiating backgrounds by sight alone is not easy. However, it is important to pay attention to different cultures and religions. What is acceptable in your culture may not be considered acceptable in other countries. It is probably best to avoid conversations about race, politics, religion or similar controversial topics with people from different backgrounds because they are quite likely not to share your own views and any conflict caused could be dangerous no matter how innocent your remarks are. Even attempts to take that person's side could potentially be taken the wrong way. Just keep conversation very neutral always to be on the safe side.

It is best to address all adults by their title unless you are introduced to them by their first name, especially people in authority. Also some older people don't like people to address them by their first name unless they are friends or relatives. If no one else is addressing the person by their first name its best to stick to their title. If they do happen to find this odd, they will invite you to call them by their first name. Better to be thought too stuffy than lacking manners. Usually when meeting people for the first time, they will specify what they like to be called. If they do not specify, politely ask them what they prefer being called.

Obviously there are a number of social situations where use of titles would be considered rather bizarre, so you wouldn't address someone taking a class with you or that you meet in a bar by their title. Usually you wouldn't address someone under thirty by their title other than in a formal scenario.

Visitors

If someone is visiting your house you have no choice but to be polite towards them. If you are the person who invited them, then when they arrive, look towards them and say 'Hello' (or even 'Hi' would probably do). Be prepared to shake hands with them if they should happen to put their hand out. Even if they don't shake hands on arrival, they might do it on departure. You only need to do this if they take the initiative, though of course you can take the initiative if you wish. Most people don't shake hands with people they have met more than once though some people do. If you already know the person they may choose to give you a kiss on the cheek, though men don't usually kiss each other. As an Aspie you may find the kissing unpleasant (perhaps due to sensory issues) so try not to make displeased comments. You would be better to instead back away and tell the person you don't like kissing. The same approach is more difficult for shaking hands as many Aspies do find handshaking unpleasant, again perhaps due to sensory differences. To refuse a handshake with someone you've just met for the first time would be deemed odd. It may be OK to politely refuse to shake hands with an individual who proves to be a persistent handshaker, as long as you explain very clearly you have legitimate reasons for it and that it's nothing personal.

If you are the host, then you could offer to take your visitor's coat and hang it up. Then offer them some sort of refreshment, usually a cup of tea or coffee. Throughout the meeting aim to make your visitor feel at home. If they are staying overnight, try to make their stay as comfortable as possible. If they are staying for a few days, an idea might be to at least show them around the local area unless you go further afield.

Churches and places of worship

This is one scenario where you certainly can not just please yourself as to what you do and don't do. During a service, you are obligated to do just as all the other people do, although of course you do not have to join in with the prayers if you do not wish to pray. At the same time, don't tell anyone that you think praying is rubbish or whatever, as there would be little point entering a church service if you have no respect for other people's beliefs. It is sufficient to simply look straight ahead while others are praying. Nobody will take offence because they will be too busy praying to notice.

Unfortunately, you would be expected to go along with the standing and sitting back down with the rest of the congregation. Even if you do not intend to sign the hymns etc., it is best to just stand up and sit down at the right times out of politeness. If you are there for a wedding, funeral or christening, you will not be the only person doing it just to be polite. If anything, you will feel uncomfortable if you are seated when everyone else stands.

In most Christian churches, there is an opportunity to take communion bread and wine. This is not something that people do because of hunger, but for religious reasons (some people might not know that!). If you follow religion then you are welcome to join the queue to take some, but do exactly as the rest of the queue do, and do not join the front of the queue if you are unsure what to do. If you are not religious, then you do not have to take the bread and wine. If you are, you are still not obligated as it is entirely your own choice. In some churches, ushers come round to ask you if you would like to take part. When they reach your row, do not feel under pressure, if you do not wish to take part just politely shake your head. Be aware that the rules differ in different areas of the Christian church, such as Catholic, Methodist, Free Church and so on.

Another aspect of Church services is that it is very difficult avoiding having to shake hands with someone. You may be thinking, 'I just came here to watch my niece get Christened and then I'll leave,' but at one point of the service, the clergyman will suddenly say, 'Clasp the hand of the person sitting next to you.' Everyone takes part in this even if they are not religious, so the person next to you will probably attempt to shake your hand. If you are looking the other way to try to abstain from this ritual, they will think you to be rude, so it is best to simply go along with it. People in the next row might also attempt to shake your hand. Be aware that some people might add something like 'God Bless you' or 'Peace and love'. Although this might seem uncomfortable and unnecessary, it is far easier to just smile and let it pass. Do not make any comments about it, which might cause offence. In a church, you simply have to respect other peoples' beliefs, even if you do not share those beliefs. Also, after the service, the clergyman is usually stood at the front door waiting to shake hands with every single member of the congregation. If you attempt to avoid this, do not be too obvious about it and if he does offer his hand, then it is only manners to shake it whether you think you should have to or not.

Whether you are part of the congregation or just visiting a church to look round, you must act with decorum at all times. What you wear should not matter too much as long as it is not something clearly offensive, but if you are wearing a hat you will probably be asked to remove it. Above all, do not be noisy in a church and do not mess around in any way. In a service, you should not speak unless absolutely necessary. Never hold a conversation during a service. While visiting speak only quietly. If you do happen to shout, your voice may well echo, and even if you think it is fun to try this, you will probably be escorted off the premises.

Other places of worship may have different expectations, which you must respect. For example, if you enter a mosque you may be expected to take your shoes off even if you are only visiting and synagogues have their own way of doing things too. Always check the rules before going in a place of worship.

Above all else, do not use mobile phones in a church and if you take one in with you, make sure you switch it off before you go in. It is advisable to have a keypad lock for your phone, which means that it can only be switched back on by keying in the relevant digits, which prevents it from being switched back on by itself. Also, do not eat, drink or smoke in a place of worship.

Libraries and museums

In some ways these are similar to churches, as you are expected not to make too much noise, and need to switch off your mobile phone. Also just like in a place of worship, you are not allowed to run. A library is not the best place to start a conversation with a stranger, as you could be distracting them and possibly everyone nearby. Again, do not eat, drink or smoke except in the café if there is one.

Cinemas

You are probably familiar with the concept of people on television speaking in a cinema and the people a couple of rows in front turning round and saying, 'Ssssh!' It is much more pleasant to watch a film when there are no interruptions from the audience, although quiet laughter is normal. There is an unwritten rule that you do not speak during a film at the cinema, although it is normal to interact with the person you have gone to see the film with by turning to look at them when something hilarious happens and laughing quietly with each other. It is likely that if your friend found the same thing funny that they will look at you also. Do not expect your partner to look at you every time something funny happens, but if something exceptionally funny happens, they probably will look at you and laugh with you about the scene.

It is OK to use the toilet during the film or go to the kiosk to buy food. Unless you are sitting at the end of your row, you should aim not to do this more than once. The other people in your row will have to stand up twice to let you get past, once when you go and once when you return and this can be a very uncomfortable and inconvenient experience for all concerned. Of course, you need to be prepared to stand up yourself if someone else needs to get past you, although this is most common at the beginning of the film. If you were assigned to a particular seat, then you need to sit there otherwise someone is likely to come along and tell you that you are sitting in their seat.

Theatres

Theatres are slightly different from cinemas. Again, don't distract the other members of the audience; some performers interact with the audience and this may involve asking the entire audience to stand up and start clapping. You could look very odd if you do not join in. Although you might feel silly standing there clapping a lot, nobody else is even going to notice you because they are all clapping too and are too busy enjoying the show to notice what you are doing. Also, the performers sometimes invite a reaction from the audience. We're all familiar with the lines, 'Oh no it's not!' and, 'He's behind you!' (in pantomimes).

Celebrations

For some people with Asperger's syndrome, celebrations can be very traumatic social occasions. Perhaps for some Aspies the worst part of this is the insistence of NTs to make some sort of unpleasant physical contact! At these events this can tend to be a bit overpowering, such as an uncle engaging you in a very firm handshake or an auntie giving you an unwanted kiss on the cheek!

Unfortunately for Aspies, there are a few situations where these social rituals are almost impossible to avoid. The one single celebration where the only avoidance strategy is to stay at home is New Year. This is the one time where everyone insists on shaking hands with or kissing everyone else and some Aspies may find this very difficult to cope with. It would be rare for the people in your company to not do one of these two things. Handshaking does not have to be too traumatic, as usually a handshake takes about one second, which means that it's over before you have a chance to worry about it. Kissing might be a bit harder to deal with, but again it does not take long. In the vast majority of cases, you will be kissed on the cheek, though your partner will usually kiss you on the lips. If someone kisses you on the lips, you are entitled to object and usually they will understand your objections.

You might also receive a kiss or handshake around Christmas or on or near your birthday but other than New Year the single social situation where most kissing and handshaking takes place is at a wedding. It is customary to shake hands with the groom and to give the bride a peck on the cheek. If you are not going to the reception afterwards you might manage to avoid this, but as either the bride or groom is obviously a friend or relative, they might feel a bit hurt if you do not at least go over and congratulate them. At most wedding receptions, the Wedding Party (i.e. the bride, groom, parents and best man) all line up and each guest is expected to go down the line and either shake hands with or kiss each person. You are not obligated to instigate any kissing, you may shake hands instead if you prefer, although some people in the line might give you a peck on the cheek anyway, and you just have to grin and bear it.

If you feel that you would not be able to face this, you could try sneaking in the room beforehand. You will probably be caught out or you could go a walk round the block and return when you feel that everyone might have gone inside, though you will either have a long wait or end up walking in late and disturbing the events, which would be embarrassing. There is no easy answer for this one. It is best to just go with the flow. If you go near the front of the queue, you will be inside the room with the trauma over and done with before you know it.

If you do not attend the wedding itself, some brides and grooms will insist on standing at the entrance to the venue for the evening wedding party. While most couples do not do this, some do and it can be difficult to avoid. Unfortunately in life, unless we spend it staying at home and hiding, we are not going to be able to entirely avoid being kissed by people whom we do not wish to be kissed by! If you do not have to be kissed by any of your family when you meet, you may, if you ever get married yourself, have to be kissed by your in-laws. Though you may manage to avoid it if you or your spouse is able to make them understand that you are uncomfortable with it. However, this does depend on the personalities involved and it may feel insulting and disrespectful to some people if they were brought up a certain way.

If it's your own wedding, you will need to be prepared for numerous people shaking hands with and kissing you. Perhaps you could discuss with your fiancé the possibility of not having to stand in a line of people to let everyone kiss you or shake your hand.

If you initiate kissing yourself, do not kiss people that you have never met before and above all you should not kiss anyone on the lips that you are not close to, unless they are a potential partner. Usually with anyone other than your partner you would kiss them on the cheek. In some social situations people do kiss on each cheek, but most people will just kiss one cheek. You should never feel obligated to initiate kissing yourself. If you are uncomfortable with it, do not do it, simply let the other person take the lead. As for shaking hands, in the United Kingdom there are very few situations where it would matter if you did not ever initiate a handshake, although in a job interview it could help you to get the job.

Pubs and clubs

It is normal to be a bit wary if you are going inside a pub or a nightclub on your own. It is best to only do so if you have arranged to meet someone in there. Always be open-minded if anyone you do not know starts speaking to you. If you allow a stranger to buy you a drink, insist on going to the bar with them to make sure there are no surprises in your drink (but don't say this out loud). You should try not to leave your drink until you have finished with it. A good strategy is to wait until after a drink until you go to the toilet. Also beware of 'rounds'. Do not join in with buying 'rounds' for a group of strangers unless you really want to, and if you do get in a round of drinks for people that you do know, make sure that everyone does not get greedy and start asking for more expensive drinks.

Be wary of strangers challenging you to a game of pool or darts. They may want to play for money and some of these people can be quite conniving and become aggressive if you disagree with the amount they claim that you owe them.

In nightclubs pay extra care – do not leave your drink unattended and be open-minded about anyone who approaches you. You do not need to be defensive towards people as they may be every bit as nice and genuine as yourself but always be aware that not all people whom at first seem nice really are. Some people are extremely good actors and actresses.

Witnessing a fight, accident or injured person

One of the things which you may be most worried about is how to react if you witness a fight, accident or injured person when out and about. If you see a fight take place, you will largely be best to stay out of the way so that you do not become injured yourself. If you do not know the people, generally, do not become involved. If one of them is someone you get on with, you could restrain that person, but do not do this if you feel that you do not have the physical strength to do so, and do not try to restrain a stranger as they might attack you.

If you witness an accident or an injured person aim to ask if there is anything you can do, but you are not obliged to get involved. Showing willing is the best thing to do if you are unsure. You may be asked to ring for an ambulance. Make sure you know what you are reporting and where you are calling from. If you see someone injured and you know basic first aid you could administer it, but if in doubt, leave the injured person alone and leave it to the professionals.

Using public transport

Buses

This is another area in which Aspies get notoriously stressed out. Usually Aspies only cope with such busy situations by conditioning themselves, as there is a great deal of sensory stimuli to interact with. At times, when using buses, trains and other forms of public transport it can be very difficult to know what to do. When travelling by bus, usually you have to pay the driver for the journey on boarding the bus. Ideally have some change ready so you are not fumbling around when there are impatient people behind you. Having notes is not usually a good idea as the bus driver often cannot change them, which can be uncomfortable. If there are a lot of people waiting, it is advisable to get as close to the front of the queue as possible provided that you do not push in front of other people as you would feel angry if this happened to you. There are unwritten rules with bus queues in that you are expected to go to the back even when where the 'back' is not clear. It is best to ask, 'Is this the back of the queue?' Otherwise aim to be early enough to be nearer the front of the queue. This way you will find a spare seat more easily and have a better chance of finding a seat on your own. However, at busy periods you may well need to settle for sitting next to a complete stranger, and you might have to get into the aisle to let them get past when they get off the bus. If you do manage to find a seat on your own, you might have to let someone else sit next to you, in which case you might need to ask them to let you out. All you have to do is look towards the aisle and say, 'Excuse me,' and they will let you off. If they do not move, this could be because you spoke too quietly, in which case speak louder and say, 'Excuse me, I need to get off please.' Do not sit on the front seats if you can avoid it, as they are reserved for the elderly and disabled. Although if your Aspieness makes you a very nervous bus passenger then you can be forgiven for using these seats – after all, Asperger's syndrome is classed as a disability whether people think that is reasonable or not.

Trains

Boarding and disembarking trains can be a very unpleasant experience for some Aspies. It may be tempting to wait at the back of the platform until the majority of people have boarded the train. However, the problem with doing this is that you are increasing the chance that you will have to stand up for at least part of the journey. There are advantages to trying to be one of the first people to get on but at least let others get off the train first.

If you are having a long journey it is better, if possible, to reserve a seat for at least part of your journey, otherwise you could be moved from your seat about halfway through your journey because someone has reserved it beforehand. Someone might be sitting in the seat next to the one that you have reserved and you might need to say, 'Excuse me, I've reserved the window seat.' That way they will let you get past to sit by the window. If they are sitting in the very seat which you have reserved but there is an empty seat next to them, then do not split hairs about this. Just sit in the empty seat, unless you specifically asked for a window or aisle seat and you need to be able to sit in one or the other for reasons related to your Asperger's syndrome. Some modern trains no longer use the old-fashioned system of inserting a ticket into the top of any seat which has been reserved and instead have electronic displays overhead which say if the seat has been reserved for any part of the journey, so keep that in mind.

Nearly all trains have overhead luggage racks. You may wish to have your bag handy for eating your lunch or getting a book. Therefore you might want to rummage around in there a few times during that journey so it might be best to keep your bag under your seat instead. This is so you don't annoy the person sitting next to you, which you might if they have to keep moving to let you get your bag down from the overhead rack.

If you make use of both the toilet and onboard shop (if there is one) during your journey it may be advisable to go to the shop on returning from the toilet to reduce disruption to the person sitting next to you. If it's someone you know, they won't mind as much if you keep moving but even they could feel irritated if you make them move too much. You could just ask them if you could have the aisle seat.

When leaving the train (as with boarding) you may feel tempted to wait for everyone else to get off first. Be very careful that you do not hesitate so long that other people have started to get on the train making it very difficult for you to get off, and make sure you have all your luggage together first!

Taxis

If you are catching a taxi from a taxi rank always join the back of the queue and follow it along. When you reach the front of the queue, you always go to the taxi at the front of the line of taxis. Some taxis are 'private hire' only meaning you must book the taxi over the telephone in advance. Just give your name, destination to and from and the time you wish to travel .

If you have any suitcases or anything else heavy the driver will usually get out of the taxi, open the boot and take the item from you to put it into the boot. He will probably do the same when you leave the taxi at your destination. Do not get into a taxi if there are already people in the taxi. Usually if you are the only passenger you sit in the back, though you are not obligated to do this. In some taxis, particularly in London and some other big cities, there is a partition between you and the driver and so you need to get into the back anyway. When this happens there is a hole through which to pay at the end of the journey. If you are making a long taxi journey, you should agree a price beforehand.

Most taxi drivers will make some small talk with you, such as, 'Where are you off to?' or comment on the weather, current news, or traffic. Don't be alarmed by this. Answering with general, concise comments is best rather than launching into too many personal details or debates. If you do not wish to talk answer very briefly and the driver should get the idea to avoid chat.

Cycling

Do not take over the road as you will annoy other drivers who may beep their horn at you. Follow the rules of the road as for drivers. Ride close to the kerb but leave a margin for safety. Do not ride on the pavement as you might frighten pedestrians, in particular children and the elderly. Do not park your bicycle inside a building without special permission, and remember to lock it up so that it's secure.

Holidays

If you are an Aspie you'll either love or hate holidays. Do not leave all your packing until the day you go away because you are guaranteed to wind up whoever you are going on holiday with and everyone will feel under stress, which is not a very good start to a holiday. Try not to leave anything behind, as everyone else will not be pleased if they have to go back home for something an hour into the journey. If you are made to do without what you have left behind, the effect this has on you could be very stressful for everyone else, not just you.

People go on holiday to get away from it all and to relax. Try to do everything you can to enjoy your holiday. Even if you cannot enjoy yourself you should not spend the whole holiday complaining and being moody because it is not fair to spoil the holiday for everyone else.

If you are on a tour, which means many strangers are on the holiday with you, for example, a coach tour, aim to be pleasant towards other travellers. This does not mean interacting all of the time, but a bit of small talk and frequent smiles go a long way. People who go on these types of holiday are nearly (!) always nice, friendly people, and many may have gone on that sort of holiday in order to make lots of new friends. Some people may wish to spend the holiday with you. If you go on the holiday alone, you may receive offers to spend your time with another person or a group of people who hate to think of you spending all of your time on your own. You are not obliged to say yes, but if you would really prefer not to, then you should refuse politely. You may even end up exchanging addresses and phone numbers with people at the end of the week, although do not turn up at their house unannounced, and be prepared that people can seem different when not on holiday. They might be less friendly. After all, most people (!) are in an exceptionally good mood when they are on holiday.

Generally, if you foresee that going on holiday has the potential to compromise the majority of your coping strategies (routines, minimising interaction, control over sensory environment, minimising group situations) it is better to be realistic about this. The worst scenario would be to get talked into holidays for fear of asserting the fact that you may not cope with them unless you are able to meet your needs. Once on holiday, it is much harder to get out of it than it would be to be upfront about your needs before hand.

Eating out

When you go out somewhere for a meal, there are usually certain table manners to follow. If you go into a proper restaurant, you usually wait to be seated and then sit at the table you are taken to. Sometimes, booking needs to be made in advance of the meal. When your meal is served, the proper etiquette is to hold your fork in your left hand and your knife in your right hand. This is to make it easier if you need to cut any meats into smaller pieces. Do not feel flustered if you forget this unwritten rule. The staff in the restaurant will not correct you, and other diners will not notice other than possibly those seated at your table. For some foods such as rice it is fine to hold the fork in your right hand as it would be very difficult to eat otherwise. If you are at an important meeting such as a business meeting or meeting your partner's parents, you need to make a good impression and it would be better to not order something which can be messy to eat, for example, spaghetti.

Shopping

All types of retail outlets, such as supermarkets, department stores and corner shops, contain a lot of sensory stimuli which Aspies could find difficult to cope with. Aim to never go rushing around a shop to get it over with as soon as possible, because invariably someone will be coming your way at the same time. This way you might go running straight into that person and if the aisles inside the shop are narrow this could cause further problems. Aim to walk around slowly and carefully to allow for anyone who may be walking towards you. If the interactions involved in shopping become so much that every time you go out shopping you fail to return with what you went out for, you need to think alternatively. This may mean taking someone along with you to ensure you cope with any interaction. Alternatively, many shops now open for more hours (such as at night or in the evening) so try shopping at those times to avoid any social difficulties.

For small purchases it may be helpful to take a few coins out of your pocket or wherever you keep them before entering the shop. It can be very difficult at times to retrieve coins once inside the shop whether this be in a narrow aisle where people keep walking past or while stood at the till when other people are standing behind you. If you want to be sure to have the correct change ready then provided that you have all the right sort of coins, you should be well prepared! It is not always welcome to pay with a big pile of pennies and shopkeepers are not obliged to accept any more than twenty pence in pennies.

The countryside

In the countryside, people tend to be quieter and more peaceful than in towns and cities. The pace of life is slower and supposedly much friendlier, and people will sometimes be more willing to help each other out. It is unlikely that they have any sinister ulterior motive for doing this, so you do not need always to be defensive. People in the countryside will certainly not appreciate it if you make too much noise or get 'in their faces', although it is not at all uncommon when walking through a peaceful village or rambling in the hills for anyone else walking past to simply say, 'Hello.' All that is required is to say, 'Hello,' back, but if you were to say 'Hello' to everyone who walked past in a large town they would either find it strange or try to work out how they know you. If you are camping, you need to be considerate towards other campers. Each campsite will have its own rules so make sure you are aware of them beforehand.

Workmen

If there are any workmen such as builders, electricians or plumbers doing work on your house, ideally make sure that you have finished using that room long before they arrive. They will not take kindly to you sneaking in for a quick shower or making a meal when they have just gone to their van to get something. Wherever they are working ideally at some point you should be at hand to answer any questions they may have, especially at first, and you should not leave the house unless absolutely necessary until any issues have been dealt with.

It may be an idea to make sure that they can have a cup of tea or coffee any time they like. If they are only there briefly then you could offer them a tea or coffee. If it is longer then get everything out ready for them and tell them they are welcome to help themselves, unless you are willing to make them a fresh cup every couple of hours potentially for a week or fortnight. Do not offer them any alcohol, and if they light up a cigarette and you do not allow smoking in your house, do not yell at them, simply ask them nicely not to smoke inside the house. Do not let any workmen into your house unless you are satisfied that they are legitimate, be it through a reference or seeing their formal identification details.

General social habits

Smoking

If you smoke, there are an increasing number of places where smoking is no longer permitted. Do not smoke in any public places unless they are designated smoking areas. Never light up in someone's house without permission. If you do not smoke and dislike being around smoke, do not criticise smokers in their presence, as this could cause strong disagreements.

Alcohol

Aim to drink alcohol in your free time only. Do not drink during your lunch break unless you can concentrate afterwards. Aim to never drink too heavily in front of your boss at a work social occasion and as a general rule aim to avoid being drunk in serious situations such as meeting your partner's parents for the first time or a job interview. In a social situation, such as a party or a night out, a couple of drinks of alcohol could loosen you up and this is fine, but try to stick to controlled situations and not become dependant on alcohol. Aim to stay in control of the amount you drink.

If you drink too much or mix your drinks it could affect your behaviour, and you risk alienating people by displaying antisocial behaviour that you do not even remember the following day. It is not the best idea to have relationships with people based on events that you do not recall, especially as by being Aspie your behaviour may be that bit more unacceptable to the majority!

Drugs

Most people don't tell you to take drugs. If you do decide to, make sure you know what the risks are and that although they may initially make you happy and relate to people better, in the long-term drug addiction makes people unable to relate effectively with people and those who care about you will find this devastating. Due to the different body metabolism of people with Asperger's Syndrome, this factor could be even more severe and it is not necessarily recommended. However, 'each to their own'. In company aim never to express strong opinions over drugs as this could land you losing friends, respect from others, and cause potentially difficult social interactions. Best to keep views neutral remembering that everyone's circumstances are different. If you have concerns over a friend's drug-taking try to angle it from the point of view of concerns about their safety rather than judgement.

Standing in queues

There are a number of situations when standing in queues is compulsory. Always join the back of the queue and do not push in even if you are in a hurry, as doing so can aggravate people quite significantly. If you are unsure what the rules are, discreetly ask someone.

Entering large buildings

If you enter the premises of any large organisation, you will usually be required to sign in at reception and in some cases report your presence to a receptionist and wait for the person you are meeting to collect you. If you are approached by a security guard, he will generally mean no harm as long as you are not wandering about where you shouldn't be or breaking the rules of the building, whatever these might be.

Calling on people

When you call at people's houses, do not bang on the door but do knock loudly enough to be heard. Do not knock too many times and if you ring the bell, do not keep it held down. Do not knock on the window if you do not know the person well as this would be considered too familiar as it is someone else's living room and they will want some privacy. If you do know someone fairly well, then just tap gently on the window.

Seeing people you know in public

If you see someone you know in the street, do not shout, 'HELLO BOB!' at the top of your voice and above all do not shout out any questions about their personal life, as they probably do not want other passers-by finding out their business. At the same time, do not make a point of crossing the road or turning a corner to avoid someone, especially if it looks obvious. It is tiring to spend your life avoiding people and most people will probably not say more than, 'Hello,' anyway.

Clothing and personal grooming

It's sad but true that society places high emphasis on clothing and personal grooming. It could certainly be a very sweeping generalisation to suggest that all Aspies have poor fashion sense and place less than average emphasis on grooming. However, if you are a logical, concrete thinker who is not particularly socially ingrained it is possible that you don't place much emphasis on outward appearance. We are not about to reel off what clothes should be worn when as it is simply impossible to think of all the situations and combinations which might occur where appearance style differs. As a baseline, whether you feel it is right or not, society expects a basic level of grooming. This means being clean, and looking after your outward health needs such as leaving any cuts dressed and so on. Basic grooming is expected to show that you show respect for other members of society rather than it mattering in a logical sense. The unwritten rules for clothing go on forever and are highly debatable and complex. The best way to look at it is dressing in such a way that determines when you need to 'play the game' or not, be this getting and keeping a job, or fitting in at a social occasion. How far a person chooses to 'play the game' or stand up for her own clothing choices is a very individual choice. However, trying to change society's majority social view over appearance is a mammoth task that often only the very brave can manage.

Cultures

If you are visiting any foreign country, pay attention to what everyone else does. Always allow the natives to take the lead. The custom of shaking hands is much more mainstream in many foreign countries than it is in the United Kingdom. Whereas in the UK it is fine to only shake hands if the other person extends theirs, there are many countries where all men and some women shake hands automatically and if in doubt it is better to join in. In some cultures you might be surprised to actually receive a kiss on both cheeks, particularly on the European continent.

Of course, beyond physical greetings, each country has its own set of traditions and rituals which all natives follow. Of course, it would take a whole book to tell you all the dos and don'ts in each different country of the world, but the good news is that even NTs can be unsure of the correct and incorrect way of conducting oneself abroad. If you are visiting an area that receives several holidaymakers who are not from that country, then the locals will be used to people not following their customs. Wherever you go, it might be helpful to go to a good bookshop and find a book that tells you how to relate to people in the country that you are going to visit.

Naturally, there will be occasions when some of the expected customs are completely at odds with your way of doing things and the natives of the country and you must not compromise your principles. For example, do not drink alcohol just to stop the natives from being offended by refusal if you are actually teetotal. Needless to say, the same goes if you are in the United Kingdom. For example, if you are at a party and a cannabis joint is being passed around the room, do not smoke it just because everyone else is. Make your own choice and do not do things that are out of character for you just to fit in with other people. You need to try to fit in with certain other things such as manners etc., but you do not need to carry out social rituals which you are uncomfortable with.

Problematic relationships

This refers to anyone you have difficulty getting on with. Try to question why it is a difficult relationship. Is there really a problem, or have things got out of hand? Can you think of anything which could make your relationship with that person more difficult than your relationship with other people? It may have been a misunderstanding. Perhaps you could talk to them about something that interests them or maybe you can involve them in something – try to build bridges somehow. Perhaps they will warm to you so try some neutral humour. Try to remind the person of the concept that they may be upset about an aspect of behaviour but that liking a person does not have to be determined by only one aspect of them.

Whether you can think of a reason for the person's bad relationship with you or not, it will pay to ask them why they behave as they do with you. No matter how negative or sarcastic the answer might be, you could always try asking if you can call a truce. Hopefully, the person will be forced to admit that really they have nothing against you, and they will then respect you for standing up for yourself. In fact in some cases this has lead to people becoming best friends. If the person provides an unpleasant reply, then they are probably just not an open-minded person and have their own set of problems. It is likely that others have a difficult relationship with them too, so it's not worth being too upset by these people. Try at least to be pleased that you tried to resolve the situation. However, there are some people with whom personality clashes will occur. There are some people you will never get on with, whatever you do, and unless you are forced into direct contact with them, stay apart wherever possible, or interact only on very neutral terms.

Criticism

Criticism is inevitable, it can be useful but it can also be downright cruel. The hard thing about it is not just what is being criticised but trying to work out what is fair and what is unnecessary. If you are being criticised try to think around what is being criticised rather than jumping in straight away with emotion. If you disagree with the criticism, provide an unemotional, assertive response. Try to show that you are trying to understand their point of view, but if you disagree make sure they are aware. If you genuinely feel that the criticism is wholly unwarranted and unkind, don't try and make the person feel it is them that you are unhappy with but rather the comment, so that you try to remove the 'comment' from your whole view of them as a person.

If you are giving criticism, social etiquette is important here. Try to be as tolerant as possible of people remembering that people grow and change and that views are not static. If you have to criticise tread carefully by giving lots of praise for things that they do well before introducing what isn't good. Don't be totally blunt but try to 'flower up' the criticism a bit by talking about a similar scenario where something hasn't worked (not relating it directly to them). If they don't 'take the hint', ask them if they think this scenario applies to them. If they don't, be more direct ensuring that they remember that it is not the whole person you are criticising but one small point or aspect of their personality.

Relating to people in authority

In life it is a basic expectation to show respect to all people, but with figures of authority, there are unwritten rules about how to relate to them. Figures of authority can include your bosses, college lecturers, doctors, police officers, traffic wardens, councillors and many others. If you are dealing with these people in their professional capacity, then you need to behave in specific ways. It is not wise to offend people in a position of power, even though in theory they are not better people than any other; logic in these social conventions goes out of the window.

As children, you were told to treat your elders and superiors with respect (perhaps!). This does not end when you enter adulthood. It is an unavoidable fact that throughout life there are various figures of authority that we cannot avoid coming into contact with, whether you agree with their position, beliefs and status or not.

In some cases, you are not welcome to address figures of authority by their first name unless you know them outside of their profession. Sometimes police officers do provide their first name in which case it is fine to address them by it, but this is not always the case, and the correct form of address would be, for example, PC Smith. A doctor who you only know professionally is almost always Doctor followed by his or her surname and in some cases you are not supposed to address your manager by their first name.

Never be familiar with a figure of authority. A little bit of polite conversation is often fine but do not ask them about their private life. The general rule goes not to flirt with them or ask them out on a date, and do not make any physical contact other than a handshake. Some professionals might occasionally pat a client on the back or shoulder, but it would be best not to do this yourself. Hugging and kissing a figure of authority is not appropriate. In many professions, it is a sackable offence to have intimate contact with a client.

You cannot usually see a figure of authority without an appointment. Therefore, you cannot just walk into the building where they work and knock on their door. You certainly cannot walk straight in nor is it a good idea to try to deal with business with a person in authority in a public place, unless they are a police officer. You should under no circumstances contact a figure of authority at their home address unless they have invited you to do so, and don't ask them questions about their personal life unless they started the conversation.

You do not need to feel terrified at the prospect of dealing with a figure of authority, as you are by no means inferior to any of them. You have just as much right to exist as anyone else. As a child, you probably felt nervous dealing with all sorts of people, especially people in authority. The chances are that someone you went to school with is now a figure of authority, perhaps a teacher, a police officer or a doctor, and this certainly does not mean that you should show them any more respect than they should show you. As long as you remain pleasant when dealing with figures of authority, there is no reason to be in awe of them or to think that they are judging you, as it would be wrong for them to do so.

Below are a few examples of some figures of authority and how to act towards them.

Teachers, tutors and lecturers

Many teachers shake hands with the parents of their pupils, particularly if it is the first time they have met. Aim to still be polite to them and not be instantly defensive each time they criticise your child. Be prepared that it is possible that they will point out areas of concern regarding your child, and that it may be something which cannot be dismissed, as sometimes things are noticed at school that are missed at home. If you are ever called into school because your child is in trouble, you can help resolve the situation much better if you remain calm and rational. The same applies if you are being given instruction or advice from a tutor or a lecturer. Try not to react emotionally if you can but try to be neutral in your thoughts and accept that they are trying to help rather than undermine you.

Bank manager

If you have an appointment with your bank manager, aim to wear the smartest clothes that you can find, as the more effort you make the more seriously he or she will take you. Make as much eye contact as you are comfortable with and be polite and courteous throughout the interview. Remain calm even if he or she refuses your request, as you may have a future appointment with him and want to be respected.

Landlord

There are two types of landlord. Indeed you should stay out of trouble if you do not want a pub landlord to bar you, but referred to here are landlords of rented accommodation. As they are giving you somewhere to stay, it would be in your best interests to be polite to them. Some landlords are unpopular with their tenants, but if you do challenge them keep it civilised and do not lose your temper, as you could be looking for somewhere else to live or have to put up with a very difficult landlord.

Religious figures

Religious figures such as vicars, priests, rabbis etc. tend to be calm, peace loving people whom take their beliefs very seriously. We all have different beliefs but we should always respect those of others. If you have dealings with any of these people then you should keep a certain level of decorum. Do not challenge their beliefs and do not use bad language or speak about crude or vulgar topics. However, this does not necessarily mean that they will have no sense of humour or insight into life outside of their religion. To be on the safe side, behave more formally than less.

Doctors and healthcare professionals

Health issues often cause anxiety, fear or upset. If you are unhappy with something that a health professional has done or said, it would not be wise to lose your temper with them as they may have information for you which is a matter of great importance to your health. There are agencies with which you can liaise should you have grievances or problems; these agencies can be found through your local health services. There are formal procedures which can be followed to deal with problems effectively. The health professional is there to safeguard your health, so do not jeopardise it by behaving inappropriately. If you do struggle to get across what you want say in the consulting room, take an advocate along with you to ensure that you get the care and advice you need.

Managers

How you treat your manager will vary greatly according to the organisation. In a large company you always treat managers with respect. It would be sensible to even treat junior managers well as they could be more senior eventually and you do not want them to hold anything from the past against you. In some companies you might be able to laugh and joke with the manager and even go to the pub with him or her. However, it would still be advisable to show them respect and to tread very carefully with your social behaviour as they are still your boss. If you treat them how you wish, it could cause a very bad working relationship and you may lose your job and even the opportunity of a good reference.

Inspectors or company directors

If you have a visit at work from someone in authority such as a manager from head office or a member of the local or county council then be very respectful towards them. A handshake would be usual, and speak only about respectable matters and do not be familiar with them. In particular, be careful to come across as well as possible if inspectors are visiting your place of work, although do not lose sleep over it. You will be fine as long as you show good manners that, as the saying goes, 'cost nothing'.

Superior officers

If you come into contact with the forces or services, for example, the army or the police force, then there are set protocols for speaking to superior officers. In some cases not only are you required to call the person 'Sir' or 'Ma'am', but you would also be required to salute them.

Gentry

If you ever meet gentry, there are various titles bestowed upon them, such as Your Grace, Your Lordship etc. You cannot reasonably be expected to always know which is the appropriate one to use, so if in doubt just use 'Sir' or 'Madam'. It is very rare that you would ever have recourse to call someone 'Madam', unless you are told at work that this is how you must address female customers.

Police officers

This is perhaps the figure of authority with whom you need to check your behaviour the most. Some police officers will arrest anyone who is argumentative with them, so if you ever have dealings with the police you should be calm and rational. Just calmly explain what happened without being defensive and aggressive towards the police officer. If you act nervously they may think you are guilty, even if you are not, so keep your composure as best you can. Do not lie to the police, particularly if you have not committed a crime, as you could become a suspect for a crime that you did not commit. It is better to make the police aware that you have Asperger's syndrome so that they can be aware should there be misinterpretations in communication.

Solicitors

Solicitors can help you for a variety of reasons. You can speak to them about any issues in which you feel you have been treated unfairly, so try to remain calm, neutral and factual in your behaviour. Do not be too ready to show anger towards your solicitor, as this could jeopardise you receiving the help that they might be able to provide. Here again, disclosing AS could be relevant.

Judges

If you are ever unlucky enough to have to appear in court then, whether you are the defendant or claimant, you need to act most respectfully. Keep in mind that any outbursts of temper could mean the difference between you been charged or not charged, or worse, going to prison or getting a non-custodial sentence. The conventions of the court need to be followed, whether they make sense or not. Again, with the Criminal Justice System, disclosing your AS could be very relevant so seek advice about this from well-informed sources.

Ways Forward and Further Support

The Missing Link Support Services Limited

For Individuals

Counselling, Psychotherapy, Social Skills, Specific Individual Support, Diagnosis, Employment Support, Training, Social Group, Social Support, Assessment

For Professionals

Training, Consultation, Workshops

For Carers

Training, Consultation, Counselling, Individual Support

Contact

www.missinglinksupportservice.co.uk

Telephone: 07971 569042

Email: vicky@missinglinksupportservice.co.uk

genevieve@missinglinksupportservice.co.uk

Asperger's syndrome Websites

Discussion Forums, Chat rooms, Real life meet-ups for AS adults in the UK and Ireland

Aspie Village

www.aspievillage.org.uk